ANTHROPOLOGICAL PAPERS

MUSEUM OF ANTHROPOLOGY, UNIVERSITY OF MICHIGAN
NO. 21

THE STEUBEN VILLAGE AND MOUNDS
A MULTICOMPONENT LATE HOPEWELL SITE IN ILLINOIS

by
DAN F. MORSE

ANN ARBOR
THE UNIVERSITY OF MICHIGAN, 1963

ISBN (print): 978-1-949098-24-2
ISBN (ebook): 978-1-951519-46-9

Browse all of our books at
sites.lsa.umich.edu/archaeology-books.

Order our books from the University of Michigan
Press at www.press.umich.edu.

For permissions, questions, or manuscript queries,
contact Museum publications by email at umma-
pubs@umich.edu or visit the Museum website at
lsa.umich.edu/ummaa.

ACKNOWLEDGMENTS

The main participants in the excavation of the mounds and the collection of surface material were Mr. George Schoenbeck, Dr. Dan Morse, and Dan F. Morse. From time to time we were helped by other persons, including Melvin Fowler, Curator of Anthropology at the Illinois State Museum; Peter Cameron, Illinois State Museum; Howard Winters, Curator of Archaeology in the Museum, Southern Illinois University; and Dr. Jose Albert, Resident Physician at the Peoria Municipal Tuberculosis Sanitarium.

In addition, representatives from the University of Michigan Museum of Anthropology (UMMA) excavated two test pits at the Steuben site from April 2 to April 7, 1956. The participants of this expedition were: Dr. James B. Griffin, Director of UMMA; Dr. Griffin's son, David Griffin; Dr. Albert C. Spaulding, Curator of Archaeology, UMMA; and the following students majoring in anthropology at The University of Michigan: Phyllis A. Morse, formerly Phyllis Anderson; Dan F. Morse; Frances O'Hara; Mark Papworth; Bruce Powell; Judy Reynolds; and Janet Stone. Peter Gibson, a student of anthropology at Beloit College, Beloit, Wisconsin, also participated in the Museum of Anthropology excavations.

Identification of the fauna from the site was done by Paul W. Parmalee, Curator of Zoology, Illinois State Museum, and the following members of the staff of the Museum of Zoology, University of Michigan: Dr. Reeve M. Bailey, Curator of Fishes; Dr. Norman E. Hartweg, Curator of Reptiles and Amphibians; Dr. Emmet T. Hooper, Curator of Mammals; Dr. Henry Van der Schalie, Curator of Mollusks; Dr. Philip Humphrey, Research Associate in Division of Birds; and Peter Stettenheim, Research Assistant in Division of Birds.

Dr. Frederick P. Thieme, Chairman of the Department of Anthropology, University of Michigan, 1957-58, assisted in the identification of the human skeletal material. The discussion of pathological conditions in the human remains is due mainly to the efforts of Don F. Dickson, Dickson Mounds State Park, Lewistown, Illinois; Dr. Ernest Elzi and Dr. Joseph Kraft, Consultants in Pathology, St. Francis Hospital, Peoria, Illinois; and Dr. Dan Morse, Medical Director and Superintendent, Peoria Municipal Tuberculosis Sanitarium.

I am indebted to Dr. James B. Griffin for his guidance during the laboratory work on the artifacts from the Steuben site, and for his kindness in editing the present paper. Dr. Albert C. Spaulding also rendered valuable help; and appreciation is expressed for many helpful hints. My wife, Phyllis A. Morse, assisted greatly in the editing of the final drafts. Plates labeled with a Museum of Anthropology catalog number were photographed by Eugene Kozlovitch; the others were photographed by Dr. Dan Morse and Dan F. Morse. A soil analysis was made possible through the help and guidance of Dr. Maurice W. Senstius, Associate Professor of Geology, University of Michigan.

Last, but not least, appreciation is extended to the owners of the explored land. Mr. Walter Crew, Chillicothe, Illinois, owns the village site, Mound 2, and the major part of Mound 1. Mr. Peter Micano, Peoria, Illinois, owns the northern one-third of Mound 1 and the other seven mounds. All of the above persons, as well as others, have helped in the excavation of the site or in the preparation of this report. I take full responsibility, however, for whatever may be wrong or misleading in the following pages.

Dan F. Morse

CONTENTS

INTRODUCTION

The Hopewell culture, called the Hopewellian Phase in the McKern Taxonomic System, inhabited most of the eastern United States from around 500 B.C. to A.D. 500. Within this period and area, prestate organized, agriculturally based societies existed in a primitive condition loosely connected by trade. The cultural phase began in the Illinois-Ohio region some five hundred years after the introduction of agriculture and pottery into this area. The strongest influences on the Hopewellian phase were received from the ancestral groups in the Illinois-Ohio area. The expansion of Hopewell culture is a story of undramatic diffusion and not of war and mass migration. But expand it did, altering cultures in its path sufficiently to show cultural relatedness, but not dominance. For a period of two to four centuries, around the birth of Christ, the Hopewell culture was at its height in magnificence; then, in most of the eastern United States, with the Southeast a possible exception, there was a gradual deterioration in those aspects of Hopewell culture which were the most elaborate. Around A.D. 500, the deterioration had changed the Hopewell culture into an altogether different phase.

Southwestern Ohio constituted the major center of influence, and appropriately enough the Hopewell site, the type site, is located there. Ohio was a center from which individuals may have traveled to the West or Northwest for obsidian and grizzly bear canines, to the North for copper and silver, and to the Southeast for mica and ocean shells. Or it may be that the prestige of Ohio was so great that these items were passed from group to group as trade items until they reached Southwestern Ohio, since between southern Ohio and the source areas there are comparatively small amounts of such items. Also, in southern Ohio are found the largest and most elaborate earthworks and a greater amount of burial furniture and retainer burials, with more diversity and more elaboration in artifacts. This elaboration indicates that the Hopewell culture was highest developed in southwestern Ohio in terms of social heterogeneity.

Illinois, particularly along the lower Illinois and the Ohio Rivers, is secondary only to the Ohio Aspect in cultural development during the Hopewellian phase. Much of the available Illinois data will be discussed throughout this paper while describing different aspects of the Steuben site; but lack of opportunity has negated a detailed analysis of Illinois Hopewell—a sorely needed treatise at this point of our reconstruction. Sorely needed because we must take cognizance of the problems confronting us, the data not now available needed to attempt answers to such problems, and rebuttals and confirmations of already published solutions.

Needless to say, once a site is excavated then the real work begins. In an analysis and interpretation of an archaeological assemblage, certain assumptions and premises exist which guide the reconstruction process. Foremost in this report is the premise that artifacts and cultures are susceptible to typological treatment. Types form the primary basis for advanced archaeological and anthropological analyses. Hence, broken fragments of pottery cluster into wares and types, and archaeological assemblages cluster into foci, aspects, phases, and patterns.

No archaeologist expects to obtain all the information concerning an extinct culture, for to excavate a site is to sample a culture. Furthermore, an excavation is merely a sampling of a site. This is due to the destructive nature of natural elements as well as to disturbances such as those caused by cultivation, construction, and artifact collectors. Hence all archaeological assemblages must be treated as samples in every sense of the term.

Interwoven into these two concepts is the fact that a site does not necessarily equal an archaeological assemblage on a component level of culture type. On the contrary, if an area was attractive for settlement once, why not again and again—especially in situations where the respective economies were similar. Hence, it is necessary either to separate the components existing at a site or to show good reason for equating site and component. Closely associated with this premise of probable multicomponency is the probable short duration of a settlement. The duration of a primitive settlement depends mainly, of course, on the relation of technology to environment. Thus factors to be considered are not only seasonal specialties of a culture's economy but also the effectiveness of cutting implements for an adequate wood supply, the relation between the fertility of land and the intensity of cultivation and/or of gathering, and others. Normally, primitive groups are rarely stationary for a long time at a site (say, one hundred years as a near maximum), but in comparison are existent much longer within an area of settlement sites. Continuous occupation at a single site for hundreds of years can not be assumed.

The word "primitive" is used in this report to indicate pre-state organized cultures. In the majority of such primitive cultures, a basic assumption is that one part of a community will reflect data very similar to another part of the same community. In other words, we assume that we are dealing with relatively homogeneous societies. Significant differences reflected in artifact assemblages are assumed to be inter-, not intra-cultural differences unless specifically indicated to the contrary by the data collected. Thus, significantly different artifact assemblages from a fundamentally identical locus suggest the presence of different cultures at different times. Archaeologists rarely conclude that two or more cultures were in the same place at the same time since this is recognized as an abnormal cultural phenomenon.

All of these assumptions are necessary to make order out of the data. They are demonstrative of the close allegiance between the main subdisciplines of anthropology. They can be left out only when the facts indicate that they are erroneous. For, all in all, we are merely assuming that we are dealing here with normally behaving cultures in normal cultural situations.

By a never-ending comparison of archaeological assemblages of similar and different content, our knowledge of extinct cultures becomes both broader in concept and more detailed in outline and development. In such cultural reconstructions, the information obtainable from a burial-village complex is highly desired by archaeologists. Such sites offer an increased possibility of obtaining a more well-rounded picture of a culture. At the Steuben site are burial mounds and a village area. In addition, this site has the added attraction of being Late Hopewell in type; that is, it belongs in the little-studied period of the apparent decline of the Hopewellian phase. The following paper is divided respectively into discussions on the physical environment of the site, excavations in the village, surface collections from the village, excavations in the mounds, and a brief summation of the total. Included in the paper are 6 figures, 63 plates, 19 tables, and 8 appendixes, as well as a list of references.

PHYSICAL ENVIRONMENT

The Steuben site is located in Sections 34 and 35, Steuben Township, Marshall County, Illinois. The site consists of a village on

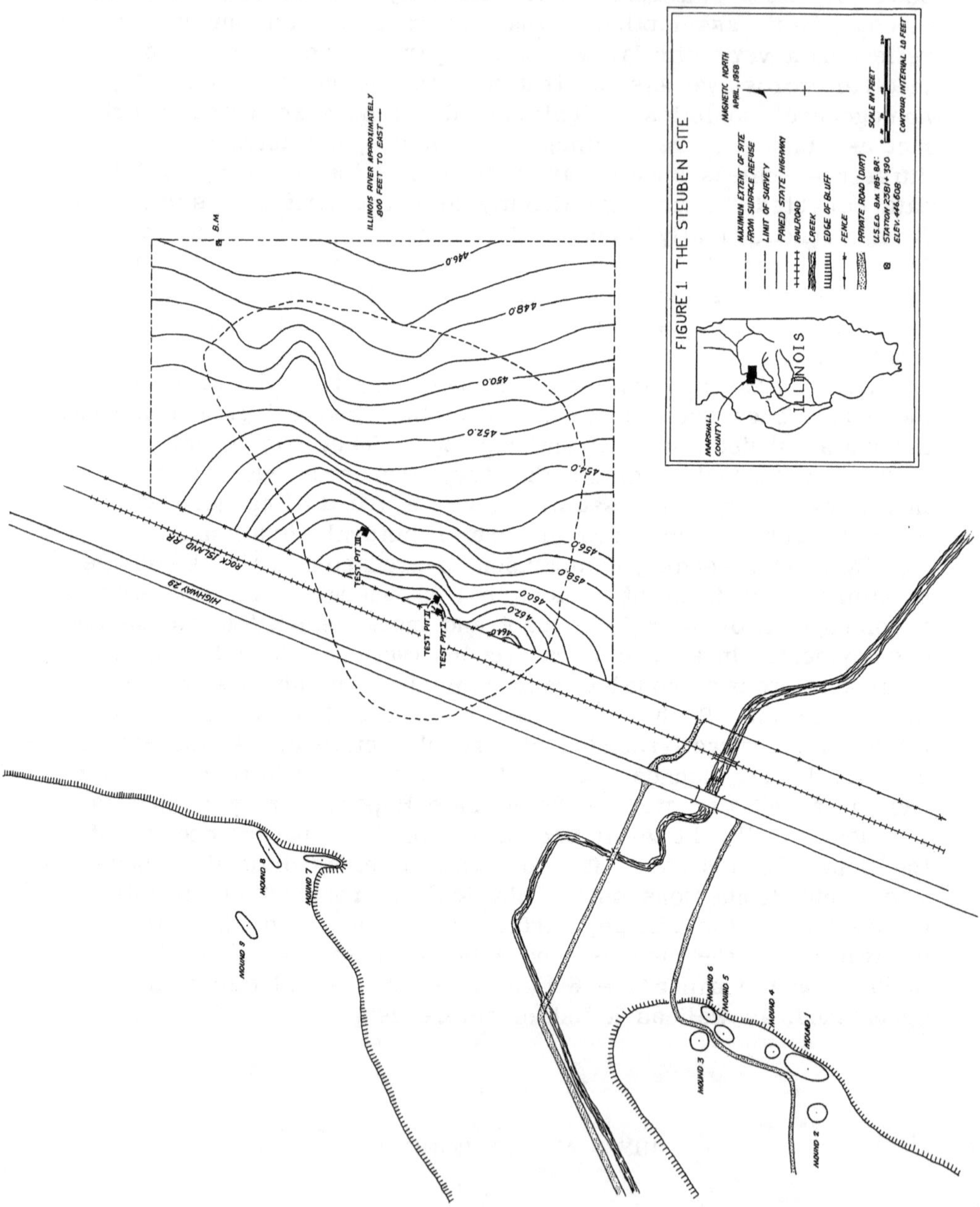

FIGURE 1. THE STEUBEN SITE

the Illinois River bottoms and nine burial mounds on the two bluffs immediately to the west. The village area is approximately nine acres in extent, and is situated between the bluffs, the Illinois River, and an unnamed intermittent creek to the south (Fig. 1). State Highway 29 and the Rock Island Railroad line traverse the extreme western extent of the village area. Two natural indentations to the immediate north and south (Meadow Lake) cause the river shore to form a semicircular boundary for this general area. The indentation to the north is not marshy. A marshy area does extend, however, from the southern extent of the northern indentation to the northern tip of Meadow Lake.

A prominent feature of the village is a ridge which runs just inside the western and northern boundaries of the site. Upon the crest of this ridge are five, six, or possibly seven mounds. These large, low mounds are most distinct to the west, in the deepest part of the site. The concentration of village refuse in these mounds could indicate that houses may have been situated on or near them.

One part of the village area is much like another in cross section (Fig. 2). The artifact-bearing zone varies from 1 to 3.5 feet in thickness and rests upon a sterile layer of yellowish brown loam. The plow zone varies between 6.5 and 8.0 inches in thickness and intrudes into a 0.8- to 2.0-foot-thick layer of mottled dark loam from which most of the artifacts were secured. Between this zone and the subsoil is a 0.5- to 0.8-foot-thick layer of yellowish brown loam which is lightly mottled with charcoal fragments and which contains relatively few artifacts. Gravel occurs frequently in parts of the site.

During the visit of the members of the University of Michigan Museum of Anthropology (UMMA) to the site in the spring of 1956, two soil samples were taken from Test Pit III to help determine its origin. Sample Number 1 was obtained at a depth of 17 inches, 39 inches east of the southwest corner stake. Sample Number 2 was collected at a depth of 51.5 inches, 45 inches east of the southwest corner stake. Both samples are essentially the same, the only significant difference being a higher phosphorus concentration for sample Number 1 due to organic waste materials in the faintly darker habitation horizon.

This soil can be summarized briefly as: (1) fairly homogeneous in profile, (2) yellowish brown in color, (3) alkaline, (4) silt loam to loam in texture, and (5) colluvial in origin. The soil type is described in *Marshall County Soils* (Winters, Smith, and Smith, 1937:14) as "Worthen fine sandy loam, bluff wash":

> Worthen fine sandy loam, bluff wash, occurs as recent deposits of sediment along the base of river bluffs in the form of fans at the mouths of gullies. Its topography is undulating to moderately sloping. It is of minor importance since it covers only 2½ square miles.
>
> This soil is extremely variable in character, the variations occurring in such small areas that they could not be shown on a map of the scale used. The color ranges from light to dark and the texture from silt to sandy loam, depending on the rate of flow of the stream carrying the sediment and on the kind of material deposited. Where the upland slopes from which the sediments are derived are not protected against erosion, coarse material may wash down in sufficient quantities to be very harmful.

This soil has the additional characteristics of a moderate drainage, the most favorable for agriculture, and a productivity rating of 3-6 for main field crops. A rating of 1 is the most productive for the state; 10 is the least productive (Winters, Smith, and Smith, 1937:Table 2, p. 27).

That the origin of this soil is from bluffs is also indicated by what are probably the two oldest dates yet obtained from a Hopewell site. Sample M-546 was dated at 25,000 ± 3000 BP, and Sample M-547 was dated at 8360 ± 450 BP. These dates have not been reported previously since they definitely do not date the Hopewell occupation. The "charcoal" was collected in Test Pit II as small fragments to be combined into datable samples for each level, thereby giving an indication of the temporal range for the site. Unfortunately, coal particles were inadvertently included with charcoal in the samples. As these two C_{14} samples were processed in the laboratory, it was discovered that sulphur was being removed, indicating the presence of coal. Several abandoned shallow coal mines are present in the bluff slopes near Steuben and the local residents, who have obtained coal from these mines for their own use, state that an extensive deposit is present.

The source of the village soil is Hennepin gravelly loam which occurs near the edges and on the slopes of the bluffs. "If cultivated, it is immediately subjected to destructive erosion" (Winters, Smith, and Smith, 1937:13). The soil immediately bordering the Illinois River consists of Huntsville loam, bottom, which is composed of recent overflow sediment. Except for the hazard of flooding, this soil is considered agriculturally good. Periodic spring flooding affects at least one-third of the village. The extensiveness of the flooding is apparently due to recent activities on the Illinois River such as the clearing of land, the construction of locks, and the regulation of the Lake Michigan source. Flooding presumably was not as extensive during the

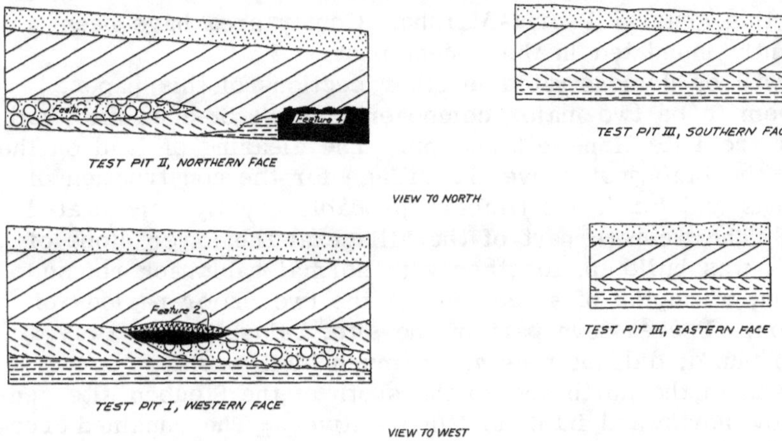

FIGURE 2: CROSS-SECTION FROM THE STEUBEN VILLAGE SITE, VIEWS TO NORTH AND WEST

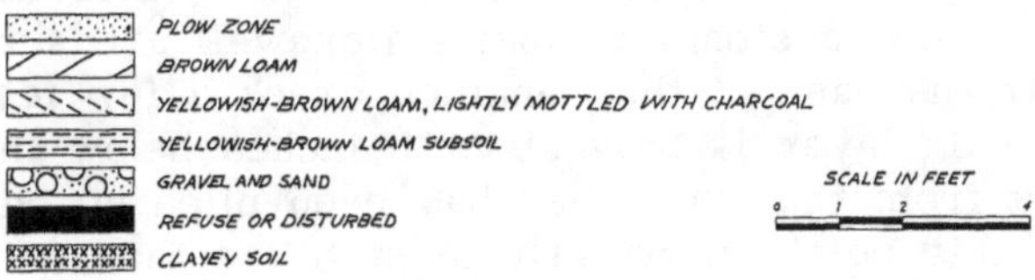

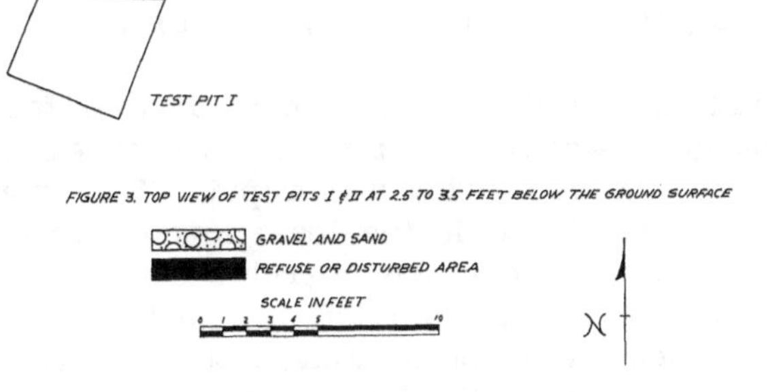

FIGURE 3. TOP VIEW OF TEST PITS I & II AT 2.5 TO 3.5 FEET BELOW THE GROUND SURFACE

time of aboriginal occupation. For instance, at least two small sites in this general Peoria-Marshall County area have been permanently inundated in the recent past.

As will be demonstrated in other sections of this paper, there seem to be two major components at the Steuben site, both of which are Late Hopewell in type. The clearing of land on the edges of the bluff just above the village for the construction of the mounds and for house timbers probably greatly accelerated erosion. The western part of the village at the lower slope of the bluffs was built up, together with normal habitation refuse deposition, to depths of 4 feet during the two major periods of occupation. The eastern part of the site, being further away from the bluffs, did not receive as much bluff wash.

Creeks to the north and to the south of the Steuben site generally flow northward into the Illinois River. The unnamed creek at the site, however, flows southward. Old maps of the unnamed creek show that its course formerly was straight east from the railroad bridge to the river. A 1- to 3-inch-water-laid layer of sandy loam with occasional inclusive Hopewell artifacts is being exposed near the base of the unnamed creek a few feet west of the fence. This layer is only about 6 inches below the surface, although dirt from the creek bed has been piled up on the northern bank at this point, apparently to stabilize the creek. Hence, this artificial overburden makes the artifact-bearing layer appear several feet deep.

Feature 1 is evidence that the unnamed creek flowed northward into the Illinois River which is normal for creeks in the area. This feature is a sand and gravel lens, varying in thickness from 4 to 6 inches, the surface of which was about 2.5 feet below the ground surface in Test Pit II and 3.0 feet below the ground surface in Test Pit I (Figs. 2 and 3). At first, we thought that the gravel lens was a house floor. With one possible exception, however, no post molds were found in association. On the other hand, this feature is very similar to the bed of the unnamed creek.

An accumulation of village sediment of up to 4 feet would be sufficient to change the course of the unnamed creek toward the south, especially if the deposition was rapid. The small amount of debris with the gravel and in the loam in the same general level is mixed as to component membership but does indicate that it consists mainly of material left behind by the older component; the gravel lens was not treated as a separate unit in excavation but was included as the basal level of the test pits. During, or immediately after, the first inhabitation of the site, the creek began to shift its course southward. The major shift probably took place during the second occupation. After the second abandonment of the site, erosion of the bluffs and consequent deposition in the village was very minor, as evidenced by the lack of any appreciable overburden. With the beginning of European plowing, some erosion has taken place in the village proper. The village mounds, referred to at the beginning of this section, may be erosional remnants of this final event.

In summary, the Steuben site is composed of soil eroded from the two bluffs immediately to the west. The soil is homogeneous. Deposition was rapid and took place primarily during and after each of the two major occupations at the site. The unnamed creek bordering the site changed its course during the periods of occupation. The Steuben site is one of a very few possible sites along the Illinois River in Marshall County large enough for an agricultural settlement. The soil is fertile and water is easily accessible.

EXCAVATIONS IN THE VILLAGE

A total of three test pits were excavated in the village. I dug one in the spring of 1955, and the other two were excavated by the University of Michigan Museum of Anthropology (UMMA) in the spring of 1956 under the direction of Drs. James B. Griffin and Albert C. Spaulding. These three test pits represent a total excavated area of about 573 cubic feet of soil.

Test Pit I (Pl. I, Fig. 1) was a 5- by 10-foot unit dug to an average depth of 4.0 feet beneath the surface. It was excavated in 0.5-foot levels with the upper two levels combined into Level 1 to isolate the plow zone. Levels 2 to 7 are the successive 0.5-foot cuts. Two features were encountered in this excavation unit. Feature 1 was the sand and gravel lens mentioned above in the section entitled "Physical Environment." Feature 2 was a small refuse pit excavated from the base of Level 4 to just below the base of Level 5, intruding somewhat into Feature 1. The refuse layer of Feature 2 was 3 inches thick, 3 feet in extent from northeast to southwest, and was capped by a 3-inch-thick layer of clayey soil. It extended very slightly into the test pit and was only discovered when trimming the wall during the final stages of excavation. The artifacts from Feature 2 thus are included with those found in Level 5.

Test Pit II (Pl. I, Fig. 2), placed only a few feet east of Test Pit I, was a 5- by 10-foot unit excavated to an average depth of 3.3 feet below the surface. An extension was made on the northeastern corner of Test Pit II, comprising an area of 24.8 square feet, and was excavated to an average depth of 2.5 feet below the surface. Both Test Pit II and its extension were excavated in the same manner as Test Pits I and III.

Several features were encountered in Test Pit II. At the base of Level 3, 2.0 feet below the present ground surface, areas of ash and bone began to appear, and at 2.1 feet below the surface a definite concentration of refuse appeared in the eastern half of the unit. Features 3 and 4, two refuse pits, were distinguished 3.1 feet beneath the surface in the two eastern corners. Feature 3, in the southeastern corner, was not excavated, but the extension was placed so as to include Feature 4. In the extension, Feature 4 was distinguished 2.5 feet beneath the surface, the base of Level 4, and was found to consist of several refuse pits which ranged from 1.0 to 2.0 feet in depth. None of the individual pits could be isolated. Feature 5 was an unexcavated refuse pit found in the northwestern corner of the extension of Test Pit II. Its apparent diameter was about 3.0 feet and it appeared just above the base of Level 3. Feature 1, the sand and gravel lens, also appeared in Test Pit II.

Test Pit III also was 5 by 10 feet in extent and was excavated to an average depth of 2.5 feet beneath the surface. An extension of this unit was made to excavate a burial whose skull appeared in the northeastern corner of the main excavation unit (Pl. II, Fig. 1). No other features, with the exception of a cache of four perforated bear canines, were found in Test Pit III. The extension was dug in two levels; Level 1 extended from the surface to the base of the burial, about 1 foot below the surface. Level 2 extended from the base of the burial into the subsoil. The extension was 4.0 by 3.0 feet in extent and was excavated to a depth of 2.0 feet.

Burials

A representative number, if not the majority of the inhabitants of the Steuben site, seem to have been buried in the mounds on the nearby bluffs. Three burials were encountered, however, in and near the village proper. Years ago, Mr. and Mrs. George Schoenbeck discovered a burial, exposed by erosion, under the railroad bridge over the unnamed creek to the south of the site. There is no additional data available.

Mr. Schoenbeck, my father, and I located a burial near the southeastern border of the site in 1954. This was a fragmentary adolescent which had been disturbed considerably by the plow. The head was oriented toward the northeast and there were some indications that it had been flexed, possibly on its left side.

A third burial was found in the extension of Test Pit III. Several of the bones had been disturbed by the plow. This skeleton was in a tightly flexed position, on its right side, with the head to the south. A female in her late forties or early fifties, it exhibited a general condition of bone growth which affected the lower limbs and the feet, hands, and clavicles. It is difficult to determine whether this condition was caused by poor nutrition or by infection. As was the case with the other two burials, no grave goods were present, although a mandible, possibly that of a male in his thirties, was found while cleaning the bones in the laboratory.

Pottery

A total of 2,693 excavated sherds are available from Steuben to show vertical changes in wares and their constituent types. These sherds were distributed in arbitrarily selected levels in five excavation units. Levels with less than 50 sherds were combined so that each level contains at least 50 sherds. For instance, only 3 sherds were found in the bottom 6 inches and only 10 and 9 sherds respectively were found in the top foot and in the next 6-inch level of Test Pit 1. This combining allows less chance for inconsistencies due to the presence of several sherds from the same vessel in a given level. There are several classifications of Hopewell sherds for Illinois. This report takes as a starting point that used by Griffin (1952). First the wares and then the types will be discussed.

At this point, however, it is best to discuss, briefly, Illinois Valley Hopewell pottery as a whole before getting involved in specifics. Primarily this is because pottery, due to its fragility and abundance, can be used as the predominant indicator of cultural change. Hence, the data from pottery may be utilized to separate Hopewell into major subdivisions. Illinois Hopewell is commonly segregated as Early or Developmental, Middle or Developed, and Late or Degenerate. A pottery tradition exists in Illinois which includes Havana, Hopewell, and Weaver wares. Early Hopewell is defined as beginning with the Havana series. Middle Hopewell began with the advent of Hopewell ware. Late Hopewell is defined here as beginning when the percentage of Weaver ware surpassed that of Hopewell ware. The reason for this definition for Late Hopewell is that Weaver and Havana wares are so closely related that a few sherds in almost any Hopewell assemblage may be classified as Weaver in type. The break between Hopewell and Weaver cultures is equated here with the complete disappearance of the Havana and Hopewell wares. Hence, the only pottery present in Weaver culture is Weaver ware, although again a very minor percentage of Weaver sherds may have some of the Havana series characteristics.

Wares

Weaver ware is the only ware found in association with the Weaver Sub-Aspect, as is its close relative, Canteen ware with the Jersey Bluff Sub-Aspect. There was no Canteen ware at the Steuben site and the northern extent of Canteen sherds appears to be from 150 to 200 miles south of Steuben. Havana, or Havana-like ware is the predominant ware of the northern Hopewell foci while Hopewell ware is a minor ware found almost only in northern Middle and Late Hopewell components. Only three wares: Havana, Hopewell, and Weaver, were found in the excavation units at Steuben. In general, these wares are easily distinguishable but, as with most contemporary artifact types within a similar class, sherds occur which have attributes of two or of all three wares. The Weaver and Havana series are very similar in appearance, even more so than the Hopewell and Havana wares, and the most widely accepted hypothesis is that Weaver was a direct derivative of Havana. In other words, Havana ware became Weaver ware, while Hopewell ware was concomitant with Havana ware. Hence, during Late Hopewellian times, both Havana and Weaver existed as major wares. If this hypothesis is correct, then one would expect a fairly gradual increase of Weaver ware and a corresponding decrease of Havana ware during this period. The data from the Steuben site substantiate this hypothesis. In addition, Hopewell ware, which was never a major ware, should be decreasing in percentage in Late Hopewell. Hopewell ware probably was mainly a ceremonial ware; it is well-made, rare, and the most common pottery included as burial furniture. Its presence in refuse pits indicates its probable use in household and in general village ceremonies.

Weaver and Havana sherds are very similar in appearance, but there are differences. In general, Havana sherds are thicker than Weaver specimens. On the majority of cord-marked Havana sherds, the cord impressions are much closer together than is the case on Weaver sherds. Havana sherds contain a greater amount of tempering material, thus rendering the surface rougher than the majority of sherds that I call Weaver. Havana seems to contain more sand and crushed quartzite as against the normal hornblendelike tempering in Weaver sherds. A few of the Havana specimens show a more random tempering material selection such as limestone, clay, hematite, flint, etc. Mica specks occur in the original clay and thus show up in most sherds of both major wares in varying quantity. In addition, if any large grit particles are present in the tempering material, the sherds, by and large, are Havana, but there are a few notable exceptions. Havana sherds have a less compact paste than Weaver specimens. Havana rim sherds are normally beveled in cross section whereas Weaver rims have flattened or unmodified rounded lips. It is interesting to note that Hopewell rims are rounded normally in cross section. Weaver vessels usually show a more constricted neck than do those classified as Havana. Decorative treatments, although in many cases obviously related, are usually distinctively different for Weaver and Havana vessels.

Hopewell ware consists of two subgroups: the Hopewell series and the Baehr series. Baehr is apparently a derivative of Hopewell, but, while retaining limestone tempering and certain decorative motifs as well as a channeled rim, it has lost the interior and exterior polishing to burnishing of Hopewell and has added some new decorative treatments such as brushing. The Baehr series seems to have been confined to late Middle and Late Hopewellian times.

Table I shows the vertical distribution of Havana, Weaver, and Hopewell wares in four excavation units. This bar graph presentation permits a visual trend in the three series to be observed. Two very basic questions, however, have to be answered on the basis of this data before any further inferences can be made.

The first question is: what is the probability that the distribution of artifacts in each test pit is or is not due to sample vagaries? In other words, do we have good representative samples? An easy test for this is the contingency X^2 technique (Moroney, 1957:246ff). Essentially, the hypothesis is made that all the samples collected came from a homogeneous situation. A significant difference between two samples is shown by getting a very low level of probability that this hypothesis of homogeneity is correct. Thus a result consisting of a very low level of

TABLE I

VERTICAL TRENDS IN THE THREE HOPEWELL WARE GROUPS AT STEUBEN

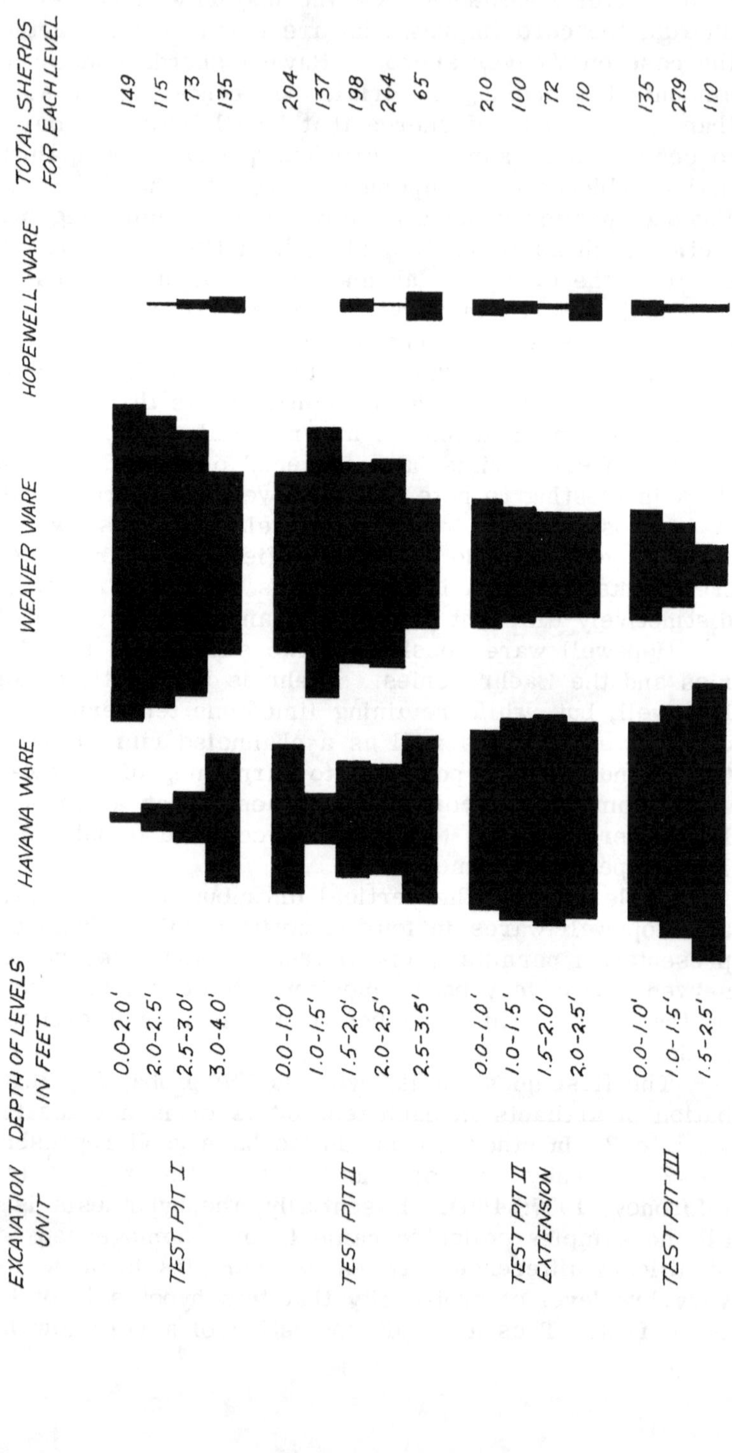

probability indicates that the samples probably were taken from a heterogeneous situation. If this happens, then another hypothesis must be substituted to account for the indicated heterogeneity. The theoretical range of levels of probability is from 0 to 1.0.

In both Test Pits I and III, a level of probability of beyond 0.001 resulted. The samples utilized were the constituent excavation levels of each test pit. The observed differences between the levels in each excavation unit, from base to surface, were a consistent increase of Weaver ware and a corresponding decrease of Havana ware. The X^2 result demonstrates that these differences are extremely significant. The result is consistent with our understanding of culture change, since artifact types in each successive level increase and decrease in a uniform direction. Increased time, evidenced by the site stratigraphy, is the inferred cause of the difference between each successive level in each of these two test pits. Hence, earlier levels differ in their artifact contents from later levels because of cultural change through time. Thus, on the basis of the data from Test Pits I and III, we may make two deductions. First, Weaver ware is increasing and Havana ware decreasing through time. Second, the components represented are Late Hopewell since there is more Weaver than Hopewell ware present in each level. All that can be inferred concerning the behavior of Hopewell ware at this point of the analysis is that it is very sparsely distributed in all levels. Test Pit I does indicate, however, that Hopewell ware was decreasing with the decrease of Havana ware.

A level of probability similar to those obtained for Test Pits I and III, also was obtained for Test Pit II. This result, however, may be due mainly to the two top levels of the excavation unit. The difference between levels 3 and 4 is insignificant, being between a 0.70 and a 0.60 level of probability. But, the differences between all other levels are significant; all are beyond a 0.01 level of probability. Surprisingly, in the upper portion of the test pit, Havana ware increases in importance. An explanation is needed for this significant increase of Havana and decrease of Weaver in the upper levels since this is contrary to our hypothesis of ware change. Possibly an aboriginal pit nearby was dug to a lower level of the site and the pit fill distributed upon the village floor in the area of Test Pit II. The village floor at the time of digging the pit was at about the base of the 1.0-foot cut. Additional evidence of mixture between levels in Test Pit II is the presence of two sherds respectively in levels 2 and 4 which fit together.

The level of probability of the vertical arrangement of wares in the extension of Test Pit II is almost 0.30. Hence, there is very little difference in the vertical distribution of wares. This is certainly not the same order of significance observed for Test Pits I and III whose results conform to the central hypothesis of ware change through time. As was indicated in a previous section, this excavation unit seemed to have a complex series of aboriginal pits included within its boundaries. Thus it seems reasonable to interpret this result as having been caused by extensive mixture tending to make the excavation unit appear very homogeneous in artifact distribution.

At this point in the basic interpretations, a common practice would be to combine either all the excavation units or at least Test Pits I and III. The cross sections made in the site show a homogeneous soil profile, thus tending to indicate over-all contemporaneity. This cannot be assumed, however, though several Hopewell sites have been so treated in the Illinois Valley. To divide a site vertically by virtue of soil zones in a normal soil profile is as arbitrary as 6-inch levels. Irregular erosion and deposition are factors which cannot be ignored. Thus, the second basic question to be asked is: were the different test pit contents at Steuben contemporary?

Test Pit III is separated from the other two main excavation units by almost 200 feet, while all points of Test Pits I and II and the extension of Test Pit II are within a distance of 8 to 34 feet. A contingency X^2 test concerning the wares between Test Pits I and III resulted in a level of probability of beyond 0.001, indicating that the chance is extremely low that these two units were from a single component. Each of the two excavation units has been demonstrated to be probably a good representative sample through time of the area excavated. Since each appears to be a sample of a different component, they probably are not contemporaneous. Table I indicates that Test Pit III is earlier since Havana ware is greater in percentage and Weaver less than in Test Pit I.

Test Pit II and its extension are also significantly different from Test Pit I, and from each other, but their proximity to Test Pit I and to each other would indicate that they should be contemporaneous. Evidence concerning the probable vertical mixture of these two units has been discussed. For instance, Test Pit II and its extension contained all but one of the aboriginal pits found in the village excavations. Now it also appears that there is some horizontal mixture present as well. The ware percentages indicate that the mixed pits fall in type between the assemblages exhibited by Test Pits I and III. The overlap of the two components is also evident in Test Pit I where the bottom foot of deposit which contains artifacts is slightly mixed, but still retains the Test Pit III characteristics of a strong predominance of Havana over Weaver ware. The extension of Test Pit III also seems to be multicomponent (Table VI, p. 29). A total of 175 sherds was found in the excavation unit containing Burial 3. Only 24 were found below the burial whereas the remaining 151 sherds were within the burial level and in the plow zone which had intruded into this layer. The large amount of Weaver sherds in relation to Havana sherds in the Burial level and the absence of Weaver ware below this level indicates that Burial 3 was made during Test Pit I times into a Test Pit III habitation area.

Hence, the data from the Steuben site so far indicate two different populations or components at the site which are characterized by Havana and Weaver being the respective major wares. Both are Late Hopewell and occupied two slightly overlapping areas of the site. Test Pits I and III, respectively, are samples of these two components. Test Pit II is an example of a mixture of both components where they overlap.

Types in the Excavation Units

Havana Ware.—The point of separation between Havana Plain and Havana Cordmarked seems to differ from individual to individual. Here, any indication of cordmarking on a sherd caused that sherd to be placed in the Havana Cordmarked type. Sherds, not vessels, are being typed and a vessel may exhibit on its exterior surface a full range from unmodified cordmarking to completely obliterated cordmarking. The main assumption, however, is that cordmarked and plain sherds respectively cluster into two types and that inconsistencies either way are relatively minor and form a balanced constant through time. It is not known whether the plain sherds are a result of obliterating a cordmarked surface or whether a smooth paddle was used during the final steps of vessel manufacture. A support of the assumption outlined here is that, in general, large sherds and complete vessels are consistent in surface treatment.

A combination of the UMMA test pits at the Snyders site in Calhoun County, Illinois, give the following indications concerning the behavior of Havana Plain and Cordmarked types (Powell, 1957). In the lower four levels, Havana Plain is at about its peak of relative frequency; while Havana Cordmarked, comprising a slightly smaller percentage of the total sherds, is increasing in importance. The increase in Havana Cordmarked continues until about the fourth level below the surface when it decreases in importance. Havana Plain in the intervening three levels has decreased until clearly secondary to its cordmarked counterpart in relative frequency. During the upper four levels, the cordmarked type has not increased or decreased significantly. The upper four levels include all the Canteen sherds, which increase greatly in importance in levels 1 and 2. The presence of Mississippi sherds in the upper four levels at the Snyders site is suggestive of disturbance, but nowhere is it much more than just a trace relative to the other sherds.

I examined the sherd counts of a select group of what are regarded as the least-mixed test pits at the Snyders site. These were loaned to me by Dr. James B. Griffin. Two distinct Hopewell components seem to be represented in the Museum of Anthropology's excavations at the Snyders site. In the test pits, with one exception which may contain a single component, one component directly overlies the other. The older component has no Hopewell or Canteen ware, and reflects a preliminary fluctuation in the Havana Cordmarked versus Plain tendency for dominance with a Havana Plain peak occurring at the end of the first occupation. Havana Zoned types are well represented and there are only a very few Fettie and Morton Incised sherds present. Sister Creeks Punctated very rarely occurs, but it is nowhere a persistent type in the Illinois Valley.

The younger component consists of a Havana Cordmarked peak, Hopewell ware which includes Baehr sherds in the upper levels, and a minor percentage of Canteen ware. Havana Zoned sherds are present but do not seem to constitute as large a percentage as in the older component. The older component is Early Hopewell in type and is related closely to Mounds 2 and 6 at Havana (Baker, and others, 1941) and to the assemblage from the fill of P°477 and 478 in the Dickison Mound group (Walker, 1952:38, Pl. XI), although the Dickison Mound fill assemblage and possibly the Havana Mounds 2 and 6 may be slightly earlier. I regard the younger component at Snyders as belonging to the latter half of Middle Hopewell. Another possible interpretation of the Snyders situation is a continuous occupation from Early Hopewell until the end of Middle Hopewell.

In Test Pit III at Steuben, Havana Cordmarked is more prominent than Havana Plain and both come to a rather abrupt end at about the same time in Test Pit I (Tables II-V). It is interesting to note that while Weaver Plain in Test Pit III is

TABLE II

VERTICAL DISTRIBUTION OF POTTERY TYPES IN TEST PIT I

LEVEL	HAVANA PLAIN #	HAVANA PLAIN %	HAVANA CORDMARKED #	HAVANA CORDMARKED %	STEUBEN PUNCTATED #	STEUBEN PUNCTATED %	NAPLES DENTATE STAMPED #	NAPLES DENTATE STAMPED %	HUMMEL DENTATE STAMPED #	HUMMEL DENTATE STAMPED %	WEAVER PLAIN #	WEAVER PLAIN %	WEAVER CORDMARKED #	WEAVER CORDMARKED %	WEAVER PLAIN STAMPED #	WEAVER PLAIN STAMPED %	WEAVER NOTCHED OR WAVY LIP #	WEAVER NOTCHED OR WAVY LIP %	HOPEWELL RIM #	HOPEWELL RIM %	HOPEWELL ZONED ROCKED DENTATE STAMPED #	HOPEWELL ZONED ROCKED DENTATE STAMPED %	HOPEWELL ZONED INCISED #	HOPEWELL ZONED INCISED %	BAEHR BRUSHED #	BAEHR BRUSHED %	TOTAL SHERDS
0.0-2.0′	1	0.7	1	0.7	1	0.7	1	0.7	—	—	102	68.4	38	25.5	2	1.3	3	2.0	—	—	—	—	—	—	—	—	149 (100.0%)
2.0-2.5′	4	3.5	5	4.3	1	0.9	—	—	—	—	59	51.2	41	35.7	4	3.5	—	—	—	—	1	0.9	—	—	—	—	115 (100.0%)
2.5-3.0′	7	9.6	1	1.4	1	1.4	—	—	2	2.7	38	52.0	23	31.5	—	—	—	—	—	—	—	—	1	1.4	—	—	73 (100.0%)
3.0-4.0′	23	17.0	22	16.3	3	2.2	2	1.5	4	3.0	46	34.1	26	19.3	3	2.2	—	—	1	0.7	3	2.2	—	—	2	1.5	135 (100.0%)

TOTAL SHERDS	HAVANA PLAIN	HAVANA CORDMARKED	STEUBEN PUNCTATED	NAPLES DENTATE STAMPED	HUMMEL DENTATE STAMPED	WEAVER PLAIN	WEAVER CORDMARKED	WEAVER PLAIN STAMPED	WEAVER NOTCHED OR WAVY LIP	HOPEWELL RIM	HOPEWELL ZONED ROCKED DENTATE STAMPED	HOPEWELL ZONED INCISED	BAEHR BRUSHED	TOTAL
	35	29	6	3	6	245	128	9	3	1	4	1	2	472

←HAVANA WARE→ ←WEAVER WARE→ ←HOPEWELL WARE→

secondary to Weaver Cordmarked, a situation also reflected in the Canteen sherds at Snyders, the reverse is clearly present in Test Pit I. With the realization that Marion Thick and Black Sand types are cordmarked and that cordmarking again becomes prominent in the Late Woodland Weaver and Bluff cultures, it is inviting to compare this with Kroeber's cyclical change in certain cultural traits (Kroeber, 1948:390ff). That is, there seems to have been a shift through time from cordmarked to plain (a Havana Plain peak) and back to cordmarked (a Havana Cordmarked peak) vessel surfaces. With the advent of Weaver, the same sort of fluctuation seems to occur; that is, there is a Weaver Plain peak followed by a Weaver Cordmarked peak. At this time, it is difficult to determine whether this cyclical sort of change is occurring in other Hopewell sites. But, if Snyders and Steuben, essentially the southernmost and the northernmost reported Hopewell sites in the Illinois Valley, reflect certain broad trends in pottery types, then Hopewell sites in between the two should reflect the same general trends.

At the Poole site, Havana Plain far exceeds any other type (Epstein, *in* McGregor, 1958:31ff; note his Fig. 16 on page 46). Amazingly enough, there is almost no variation through time. Havana (and Poole) Cordmarked is rare and there are no Weaver Cordmarked sherds present. The surface finish of Havana Plain is defined as "exterior more or less smoothed" (McGregor, 1958: 212). This then could imply that a number of sherds which I would classify as Havana Cordmarked were called Havana Plain. At the Irving site, "across McKee Creek from the Poole Site," cordmarked types predominate in every category (Taylor, *in* McGregor, 1958:67, Fig. 20). It may be significant to note that two different individuals worked with the pottery from the two sites. This would explain why so many plain sherds were found at Poole and not at Irving. The data presented for the Irving site strongly suggest at least two distinct components. One is obviously Late Hopewell and the other probably dates around Early to Middle Weaver in time. The Poole site also seems to be multicomponent and I suspect that one component dates around the beginning of Middle Hopewell, or possibly earlier, and that another is around the end of Middle Hopewellian times.

The Clear Lake site is similarly difficult to interpret (Fowler, 1952). An assumption here, apparently, is that while there is mixture between various levels this mixture was relatively unimportant and was more or less confined within the major soil zones. The curious behavior of the various pottery categories presumably may be due to mixture, in addition to the extremely small samples from the various levels. That mixture occurred is readily inferred from the occurrence of Canton ware with Weaver and Havana wares in the upper levels. Canton ware is associated with Maples Mills or a related focus in the Effigy Mound Aspect, Late Woodland phase, and is partly contemporaneous with Old Village-like material in the area around A.D. 9-1200. Liverpool ware, Black Sand focus, Unnamed Aspect, Early Woodland phase, dating around 500-1000 B.C., is associated with Weaver, Havana, and Hopewell wares in the lower levels at Clear Lake.

While Havana is the minority ware in reference to Weaver for the excavation units at Clear Lake, Havana Plain predominates as a whole over Havana Cordmarked. The same sort of predominance is also true of Weaver Plain. Certain indications are present in the report that the criteria used in differentiating plain from cordmarked are similar to mine. Probably more than one Hopewell component is present. At the Clear Lake site, there are at least two pre-Hopewell components, and probably more as indicated by the projectile points. Post-Hopewell components certainly include at least one Mississippi focus, a Maples Mills focus, and probably at least one Weaver focus. That more than one Hopewell focus is present surely is amply indicated by the fact that all of the sherds illustrated in Griffin's article "Some Early and Middle Woodland Pottery Types in Illinois," were collected at the Clear Lake site (Griffin, 1952:96, footnote).

The Havana site is another possible example of a multicomponent site being interpreted as essentially reflecting one occupation (McGregor, 1952). Havana Plain is proportionally dominant throughout the three levels of the combined excavation units and doesn't seem to drastically increase or decrease through time. The sherds and vessels from Havana Mounds 2 and 6, as stated before, are similar to the sherds from the mound fill at Dickison and to those in the older Snyders assemblage, and seem to belong in Early Hopewell. The same sort of assemblage may have occurred in the village level beneath F°54 (Cole and Deuel, 1937: 159). This essentially Early Hopewell pottery assemblage should not have any Hopewell ware in association. McGregor states, however, that ". . . they [Havana Stamped, Hopewell Incised, and Baehr Zoned] were found most commonly in Mound 6 which seems to be about the latest mound and horizon at this site" (1952:82). This statement makes little sense in light of what has been published elsewhere on Mound 6 at Havana and what has been found at other sites in the Illinois Valley. Mound 6 was excavated by Taylor in 1927 (Moorehead, and others, 1928:160-62) and redug in

1945 by the Illinois State Museum. "In spite of Moorehead's suggestion that much still remained in the mound, only a few sherds were found in 1945" (McGregor, 1952:50). Perhaps either the earlier quote from McGregor (1952:82) contains a typographical error or the sherds were in Taylor's backfill.

The suggestion made here of the cyclical behavior of the Havana Plain and Cordmarked types in at least the lower half of the Illinois Valley differs from a previous speculation. Griffin suggests a geographical (tribal) difference between the lower and the central Illinois Valley in terms of the predominance of plain or cordmarked types (1952:104). If, however, there is a break between the two components at Snyders, then the earlier components at Clear Lake, Havana, and at Poole may be equated with a cycle during which Havana Plain predominates over Havana Cordmarked. Other sherds and artifacts from these sites also suggest this multicomponent possibility.

In Test Pit III at the Steuben site, ten Havana sherd types are represented as compared to only five for Test Pit I. The five types not held in common are Havana Zoned Incised, Havana Zoned Dentate Stamped, Havana Zoned Plain Rocked Stamped, Havana Zoned Punctated, and Havana Rocked Dentate Stamped. That these particular Havana sherds, especially the zoned specimens, are found in an earlier Late Hopewell context but not in a later one conforms with evidence gathered elsewhere in the Illinois Valley, where they are usually placed into a Middle Hopewell or earlier context.

Since the behavior, through time, of the Naples and Hummel Stamped "types" is similar, both categories probably belong in a single type. The only difference between Naples and Hummel Stamped is that the former is a straight stamped unit and the latter a curved stamped unit (Pl. II, Fig. 2). The individual unit stamped is long and slender in shape, and may be either plain or dentated. However, there do appear to be two types of Naples Stamped (also reflected in the Hummel Stamped series) apart from the plain and dentate varieties. Only one of these two main types is represented in both of the components at Steuben. At the Steuben site, Naples Dentate sherds all have a slightly bowed-out upper rim upon which a horizontal series of vertical rows of dentate or plain stamped units are exhibited. The vessel shape and the rim treatment are identical to Steuben Punctated and the two are very obviously related. Both the Naples and Hummel Stamped varieties are sparsely represented and, it would seem, decreasing in relative importance. The other main type of Naples Stamped exhibits a series of horizontal rows consisting of vertical or horizontal units of dentate or plain stamping. The horizontal rows are separated by a space or an incised line. Exterior nodes are common, many times the lip is notched, and the whole design is generally on the lower rim and upper shoulder of the vessel. This type is as closely related to Havana Zoned as it is to the other main Naples-Hummel Stamped type. It is also the earlier of the two in time, as inferred from its presence at Snyders and other sites in the Illinois Valley. The Steuben or simple type of Naples-Hummel Stamped seems to be a late development, probably around the end of Middle Hopewell times. The Snyders or complex type of Naples-Hummel Stamped also seems to exist in time with Naples Ovoid Stamped and Neteler Crescent Stamped forms which are almost nonexistent at the Steuben site.

Steuben Punctated (Pl. III, Fig. 1) as inferred from Test Pits I and III, first increases, reaches a peak, and then decreases in relative importance. The peak of popularity apparently occurred in time during the break between the two components. The number of sherds present however, may be too few for such an interpretation, and this type may have been merely of similar minor importance throughout the time period of each component. Five of the sherds from Test Pit II have a paste similar to Weaver (Pl. III, Fig. 2). One of these is from the 1.0-1.5-foot level and has punctates below a cord-wrapped stick treatment on the lip. Another sherd, from the 0.5-1.0-foot level, has one row of punctates just below the lip. One of the Steuben Punctated sherds from the upper or burial level of the extension of Test Pit III is similar to Weaver in paste and has a single row of punctates just below the lip.

The Havana Random Punctated sherd from the 1.0-1.5-foot level in Test Pit II seems to exhibit a combination of Steuben Punctated and Hopewell Rim decorative treatments. This punctated rim sherd has a slightly beveled lip and a slight bulging effect on the exterior surface of the upper rim without a corresponding concavity on the inner surface. At the Steuben site, Steuben Punctated and Naples Stamped, as well as related types, exhibit a slight bulging of the upper one-half to two-thirds of the upper rim area over which the decorative treatment is found, but this bulging is also reflected on the interior surface. The vessel from which the Havana Random Punctated sherd came would show, also, a larger shoulder diameter in relation to its maximum rim diameter than is usually the case with most Havana types, with the exception of Havana Zoned Stamped types. The ratio of shoulder to rim diameter is more in accord with Hopewell ware jar

TABLE III

VERTICAL DISTRIBUTION OF POTTERY TYPES IN TEST PIT II

HAVANA WARE

LEVEL	HAVANA PLAIN		HAVANA CORDMARKED		STEUBEN PUNCTATED		NAPLES DENTATE STAMPED		HUMMEL DENTATE STAMPED		HAVANA ZONED DENTATE STAMPED		VICTORY BRUSHED		HAVANA RANDOM PUNCTATED	
	#	%	#	%	#	%	#	%	#	%	#	%	#	%	#	%
0.0-1.0'	31	15.2	48	23.5	8	3.9	1	0.5	1	0.5	—	—	1	0.5	—	—
1.0-1.5'	10	7.3	7	5.1	1	0.7	1	0.7	—	—	—	—	1	0.7	1	0.7
1.5-2.0'	19	9.7	41	20.8	1	0.5	1	0.5	5	2.5	3	1.5	—	—	—	—
2.0-2.5'	32	12.1	40	15.1	5	23	—	—	2	0.8	11	4.2	—	—	—	—
2.5-3.5'	10	15.4	15	23.2	2	3.1	3	4.6	3	4.6	—	—	—	—	—	—
TOTAL SHERDS	102		151		18		6		11		14		2		1	

WEAVER WARE

LEVEL	WEAVER PLAIN		WEAVER CORDMARKED		WEAVER NOTCHED OR WAVY LIP		WEAVER PUNCTATED LIP		WEAVER INCISED		WEAVER MISC. PUNCTATED	
	#	%	#	%	#	%	#	%	#	%	#	%
0.0-1.0'	61	29.9	47	23.0	3	1.5	1	0.5	—	—	1	0.5
1.0-1.5'	71	51.9	41	30.0	3	2.2	—	—	—	—	—	—
1.5-2.0'	76	38.2	41	20.8	5	2.5	—	—	—	—	—	—
2.0-2.5'	94	35.5	68	25.7	7	2.7	—	—	1	0.4	—	—
2.5-3.5'	13	20.0	11	16.9	2	3.1	—	—	—	—	—	—
TOTAL SHERDS	315		208		20		1		1		1	

HOPEWELL WARE

LEVEL	HOPEWELL RIM		HOPEWELL RED FILMED		HOPEWELL PLAIN		HOPEWELL ZONED DENTATE STAMPED		HOPEWELL ZONED ROCKED DENTATE STAMPED		HOPEWELL ZONED INCISED		BAEHR BRUSHED		MONTEZUMA PUNCTATED		TOTAL SHERDS
	#	%	#	%	#	%	#	%	#	%	#	%	#	%	#	%	
0.0-1.0'	—	—	—	—	1	0.5	—	—	—	—	—	—	—	—	—	—	204 (100.0%)
1.0-1.5'	—	—	—	—	1	0.7	—	—	—	—	—	—	—	—	—	—	137 (100.0%)
1.5-2.0'	—	—	2	1.0	—	—	—	—	1	0.5	1	0.5	1	0.5	1	0.5	198 (100.0%)
2.0-2.5'	2	0.8	1	0.4	—	—	—	—	—	—	—	—	—	—	—	—	264 (100.0%)
2.5-3.5'	—	—	—	—	1	1.5	2	3.1	1	1.5	1	1.5	1	1.5	—	—	65 (100.0%)
TOTAL SHERDS	2		3		3		2		2		2		2		1		868

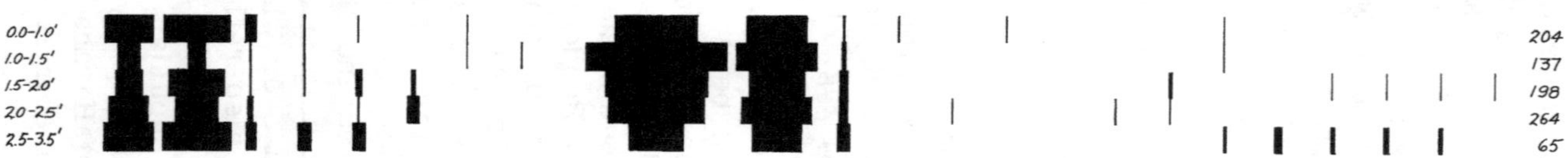

forms and with some of the Weaver vessels. The decoration on this sherd consists of a continuous area of overlapping, randomly placed, shallow, and vertical oval punctates. Immediately below this area and just at the base of the bulge is a row of evenly spaced, deeper circular punctates. Thus, the sherd seems to belong to that Havana series consisting of a jar shape, a zoned, stamped rim treatment, and a zoned, or unzoned, stamped body treatment. The careless execution, in relation to other specimens from Steuben and elsewhere, might indicate that this artifact represents the final attempts of survival for the series.

Victory Brushed is a name given to Havana Plain sherds exhibiting coarse and irregular lines. The brushing marks on the exterior surface, apparently caused by a bundle of twigs, were perhaps a function of the smoothing process or a Havana counterpart to Baehr Brushed. This category is not prominent anywhere in the Illinois Valley.

Weaver Ware (Pl. IV, Fig. 1).—The Weaver Plain and Cordmarked sherd types have already been discussed. Other Weaver types are not numerous nor are they represented by very many sherds. Weaver Plain Stamped occurred only in Test Pit I, thereby suggesting that the type is late.

One of the sherds of Weaver With Notched or Wavy Rim from the 2.0-2.5-foot level of Test Pit II exhibits a brushed exterior surface which is somewhat similar to Victory Brushed. A Weaver rim from the 1.0-1.5-foot level of Test Pit II shows an attempt to drill a repair hole on the exterior plain surface.

The Weaver Incised sherd from Test Pit II, 2.0-2.5-foot level, has broad incisions in the form of arcs ending at the intersections. The otherwise plain-surfaced body sherd exhibits parts of three such joined arcs within each other. Whether the apexes of the arcs are up or down in relation to the vessel is not determinable.

The Weaver Random Punctated rim sherd from Test Pit II, in the 0.5-1.0-foot level, has a cordmarked surface treatment upon which is superimposed a rectangular block of three horizontal rows of deep, round punctates just below the lip. Each row consists of at least five punctates up to the place where the sherd is broken. The rounded lip, at this point, is elevated slightly, almost to the place where a handle would be on a Mississippi vessel. It is very doubtful, however, that a handle existed on the vessel since handles and effigies applied to vessel rims do not appear in this area until Mississippi-influenced Maples Mills material is present. A castellation, or possibly a spoutlike outward thrust may have been present on the vessel. On the other hand,

TABLE IV

VERTICAL DISTRIBUTION OF POTTERY TYPES IN TEST PIT II EXTENSION

LEVEL	HAVANA PLAIN		HAVANA CORDMARKED		STEUBEN PUNCTATED		NAPLES DENTATE STAMPED		HUMMEL DENTATE STAMPED		HAVANA ZONED PLAIN ROCKED STAMPED		HAVANA ZONED INCISED		HAVANA ZONED DENTATE STAMPED		WEAVER PLAIN		WEAVER CORDMARKED		WEAVER NOTCHED OR WAVY LIP		HOPEWELL RIM		HOPEWELL RED FILMED		HOPEWELL PLAIN		HOPEWELL ZONED DENTATE STAMPED		HOPEWELL ZONED PLAIN ROCKED STAMPED		HOPEWELL ZONED DENTATE ROCKED STAMPED		HOPEWELL ZONED CORD-WRAPPED STICK STAMPED		HOPEWELL ZONED INCISED		BAEHR BRUSHED		TOTAL SHERDS
	#	%	#	%	#	%	#	%	#	%	#	%	#	%	#	%	#	%	#	%	#	%	#	%	#	%	#	%	#	%	#	%	#	%	#	%	#	%	#	%	
0.0-1.0'	54	25.6	45	21.4	5	2.4	4	1.9	1	0.5	2	1.0	1	0.5	5	2.4	34	16.2	50	23.7	1	0.5	–	–	–	–	3	1.4	–	–	1	0.5	–	–	1	0.5	2	1.0	1	0.5	210 (100.0%)
1.0-1.5'	22	22.0	32	32.0	3	3.0	2	2.0	–	–	–	–	1	1.0	3	3.0	17	17.0	17	17.0	–	–	–	–	–	–	1	1.0	–	–	–	–	–	–	–	–	–	–	2	2.0	100 (100.0%)
1.5-2.0'	2	2.8	41	56.9	1	1.4	–	–	3	4.2	–	–	1	1.4	–	–	10	13.9	13	18.0	–	–	–	–	–	–	–	–	–	–	–	–	1	1.4	–	–	–	–	–	–	72 (100.0%)
2.0-2.5'	25	22.7	37	33.8	–	–	–	–	1	0.9	–	–	–	–	4	3.6	17	15.4	18	16.4	–	–	1	0.9	1	0.9	–	–	2	1.8	1	0.9	–	–	–	–	2	1.8	1	0.9	110 (100.0%)

TOTAL SHERDS	HAVANA PLAIN	HAVANA CORDMARKED	STEUBEN PUNCTATED	NAPLES DENTATE STAMPED	HUMMEL DENTATE STAMPED	HAVANA ZONED PLAIN ROCKED STAMPED	HAVANA ZONED INCISED	HAVANA ZONED DENTATE STAMPED	WEAVER PLAIN	WEAVER CORDMARKED	WEAVER NOTCHED OR WAVY LIP	HOPEWELL RIM	HOPEWELL RED FILMED	HOPEWELL PLAIN	HOPEWELL ZONED DENTATE STAMPED	HOPEWELL ZONED PLAIN ROCKED STAMPED	HOPEWELL ZONED DENTATE ROCKED STAMPED	HOPEWELL ZONED CORD-WRAPPED STICK STAMPED	HOPEWELL ZONED INCISED	BAEHR BRUSHED	TOTAL
	103	155	9	6	5	2	3	12	78	98	1	1	1	4	2	2	1	1	4	4	492

← HAVANA WARE → ← WEAVER WARE → ← HOPEWELL WARE →

although Weaver in paste, this sherd may not be Hopewell. Weaver ware survives until about Maples Mills times.

In the 0.5-1.0-foot level of Test Pit II a sherd was found, possibly from a bowl, which is here called "Weaver With Punctated Lip." The lip has a row of evenly spaced, deep, circular punctates, with the center of one punctate .05 of an inch from the center of the next. Both surfaces are rough, due to grit particles breaking through. The exterior surface is plain with some plain stamping present which is probably due to a plain paddle surface treatment. Dr. Richard MacNeish pointed out to me that this decorative treatment was found on several Lewis sherds at Kincaid, where they are called "punched lips" (Cole and others, 1951:179). The "punched lip" decoration at Kincaid is associated most frequently with Type VI pottery which ". . . is found only in the last stages of the Lewis occupation. . . ." (*ibid.*, p. 181).

The Weaver Other category in Test Pit III includes the following three sherds. In the 0.5-1.0-foot level, a Weaver Plain sherd was found which exhibits a Hopewell-like channeled rim. An otherwise plain-surfaced sherd from the 2.0-2.5-foot level has a row of diagonal lines on the upper rim, not a true cross-hatched design, with a horizontal row of circular punctates immediately below. The third sherd is Weaver in paste, plain-surfaced for the most part, and exhibits a Hopewell-like dentate stamped upper rim with at least two horizontal rows of circular punctates immediately below. These three sherds are considered to reflect Hopewell ware ancestry.

Hopewell Ware (Pl. IV, Fig. 2).—As expected, there are not very many Hopewell sherds represented. Test Pit III has more sherds representing more types than Test Pit I. In Test Pit III were found examples of Hopewell Plain, Hopewell Plain Rocked Stamped, and Hopewell Zoned Plain Rocked Stamped; whereas Baehr Brushed was found exclusively in Test Pit I. Both test pits contained sherds representing Hopewell Rim, Hopewell Zoned Rocked Dentate, and Hopewell Zoned Incised types. As stated earlier in this report, there are good indications that the burial in the extension of Test Pit III was made outside of the latest Hopewell village limits into an area occupied by the earliest Hopewell component. It is noteworthy in this regard that the Baehr Brushed sherd found in this extension comes from the upper or Burial level. Hopewell ware, as a whole, seems to be decreasing in popularity in Test Pit I. The apparent slight increase in Test Pit III of Hopewell ware is probably not a true reflection of what actually occurred.

TABLE V

VERTICAL DISTRIBUTION OF POTTERY TYPES IN TEST PIT III

HAVANA WARE

LEVEL	HAVANA PLAIN #	%	HAVANA CORDMARKED #	%	STEUBEN PUNCTATED #	%	NAPLES DENTATE STAMPED #	%	HUMMEL DENTATE STAMPED #	%	HAVANA ZONED INCISED #	%	HAVANA ZONED DENTATE STAMPED #	%	HAVANA ZONED PLAIN ROCKED STAMPED #	%	HAVANA ZONED PUNCTATED #	%	HAVANA ROCKED DENTATE STAMPED #	%
0.0-1.0'	33	24.5	43	31.9	4	3.0	–	–	2	1.5	–	–	1	0.7	–	–	–	–	–	–
1.0-1.5'	62	22.2	116	41.7	5	1.8	5	1.8	11	3.8	1	0.4	–	–	–	–	1	0.4	1	0.4
1.5-2.5'	35	31.8	41	37.3	1	0.9	6	5.5	6	5.5	–	–	2	1.8	1	0.9	2	1.8	–	–
TOTAL SHERDS	130		200		10		11		19		1		3		1		3		1	

WEAVER WARE

LEVEL	WEAVER PLAIN #	%	WEAVER CORDMARKED #	%	WEAVER NOTCHED OR WAVY LIP #	%	WEAVER OTHER #	%
0.0-1.0'	20	14.8	25	18.6	–	–	1	0.7
1.0-1.5'	24	8.5	49	17.5	1	0.4	–	–
1.5-2.5'	10	9.1	2	1.8	–	–	2	1.8
TOTAL SHERDS	54		76		1		3	

HOPEWELL WARE

LEVEL	HOPEWELL RIM #	%	HOPEWELL PLAIN #	%	HOPEWELL PLAIN ROCKED STAMPED #	%	HOPEWELL ZONED ROCKED DENTATE STAMPED #	%	HOPEWELL ZONED PLAIN ROCKED STAMPED #	%	HOPEWELL ZONED INCISED #	%	TOTAL SHERDS
0.0-1.0'	2	1.5	1	0.7	1	0.7	1	0.7	1	0.7	–	–	135 (100.0%)
1.0-1.5'	–	–	1	0.4	1	0.4	–	–	–	–	1	0.4	279 (100.0%)
1.5-2.5'	1	0.9	1	0.9	–	–	–	–	–	–	–	–	110 (100.0%)
TOTAL SHERDS	3		3		2		1		1		1		524

TABLE VI

POTTERY TYPES FROM THE EXTENSION OF TEST PIT III AT THE STEUBEN SITE

Type	In and Above Burial Level	Below Burial Level	Total
Havana Plain	24	6	30
Havana Cordmarked	45	13	58
Naples Dentate Stamped	7	-	7
Steuben Punctated	2	1	3
Hummel Dentate Stamped	2	1	3
Havana Plain Rocked Stamped	1	1	2
Total Havana Ware	81	22	103
Weaver Plain	31	-	31
Weaver Cordmarked	35	-	35
Total Weaver Ware	66	-	66
Hopewell Zoned Incised	1	-	1
Hopewell Plain Rocked Stamped	1	-	1
Hopewell Zoned Dentate Rocked Stamped	-	1	1
Hopewell Dentate Rocked Stamped	-	1	1
Baehr Brushed	1	-	1
Hopewell Red Filmed	1	-	1
Total Hopewell Ware	4	2	6
Total sherds	151	24	175

Types in Feature 4

A total of 162 sherds was collected in Feature 4 at the base of the extension of Test Pit II. Of 81 Havana sherds, 44 and 27 are respectively Havana Cordmarked and Havana Plain. The remaining 10 Havana sherds are: 4 Havana Zoned Dentate Stamped, 3 Steuben Punctated, 2 Naples Dentate Stamped, and 1 Hummel Dentate Stamped. One of the Steuben Punctated sherds is similar to Weaver in paste and consists of one row of punctates just below the lip.

A total of 77 Weaver sherds includes 39 Weaver Cordmarked, 34 Weaver Plain, 3 Weaver Notched or Wavy Rim, and 1 Weaver Incised. The Weaver Incised body sherd has a slightly obliterated brushing, somewhat similar to Baehr Brushed, on an otherwise plain surface, and exhibits portions of two incised lines. The incised lines appear to be part of a geometric design of some sort which is not like the Weaver Incised sherd from Test Pit II. One line is straight and the other curved with each running along one of the broken edges toward the other.

The remaining four sherds are Hopewell Red Filmed, Hopewell Zoned Plain Rocked Stamped, Hopewell Zoned Punctated, and Baehr Brushed. The shape of the portion of the feature exposed indicates the presence of at least two, and probably more, refuse pits. The included pottery, half Havana and half Weaver, strongly suggests mixture of the two main Steuben Site Hopewell components as has been suggested for the whole of the extension of Test Pit II.

Other Ceramic Artifacts

A small and irregularly shaped chunk of fired grit-tempered pottery was found in the extension of Test Pit II. This may be a fragment of discard from the manufacture of a vessel which was accidentally burnt. Or it possibly may be a fragment of daub. Apparent daub fragments are found in a small area of the Twenhofel site near Carbondale, Illinois, as if from a house site. Since the Twenhofel site is multicomponent, especially in the general area where the daub is present, and permission to investigate further was not granted to representatives of the University of Michigan Museum of Anthropology in 1952, it is not known if the house is definitely Hopewell.

Projectile Points

A total of only 22 complete and fragmentary projectile points was found in the excavation units. Not all of the types represented in the Steuben site collection as a whole were found in the test pits, and the few points found in the excavations are not plentiful enough to indicate significant trends in the temporal changes of types (Table VII). A description of the categories represented at Steuben is in the discussion regarding projectile points found on the surface of the village.

The only Snyders Corner Notched point was found in the 1.0-1.5-foot level in Test Pit III. The two Steuben Expanded Stemmed points of the variety long and slender, and the closely related Contracting and Straight Stemmed point, variety straight base, were found in and below the 1.5-2.0 level in Test Pits I and II. The four Marshall Barbed points, variety fine, were present in all the excavation units except Test Pit III. The specimen from the extension of Test Pit III was in the upper disturbed level. The Marshall Barbed specimen from the extension of Test Pit III has

TABLE VII

FLINT PROJECTILE POINTS AND DRILLS FROM THE VILLAGE EXCAVATIONS AT THE STEUBEN SITE

Projectile Point and Drill Category	Excavation Unit												Total
	Test Pit I			Test Pit II		Test Pit II Extension				Test Pit III		Test Pit III Extension	
	Levels			Levels		Levels				Levels		Level	
	3	4	5	1	4	1	2	3	F1	1	2	1	
Snyders Corner Notched	-	-	-	-	-	-	-	-	-	-	1	-	1
Marsha'l Barbed, variety fine	-	1	-	-	1	-	1	-	-	-	-	1	4
Steuben Expanded Stemmed, variety long and slender	-	-	1	-	1	-	-	-	1	-	-	-	3
Steuben Expanded Stemmed, variety small and thin	-	-	-	-	1	-	-	-	-	-	-	-	1
Large Side Notched, variety straight and concave base	-	-	-	2	1	-	-	-	-	-	-	-	3
Contracting and Straight Stemmed, variety pointed base	-	-	-	-	-	-	1	-	-	-	-	-	1
Contracting and Straight Stemmed, variety rounded base	-	-	-	-	-	1	-	-	-	-	-	-	1
Contracting and Straight Stemmed, variety straight base	1	-	-	-	-	-	-	-	-	-	-	-	1
Small Triangular	-	-	-	-	-	-	-	-	-	1	-	1*	2
Unidentifiable broken projectile points and drills	-	-	-	1	-	1	-	1	-	3	-	1*	7
Total	1	1	1	3	4	2	2	1	1	4	1	3	24

*An asterisk (*) marks each category which includes one drill.

a slightly ground base, and the one from Test Pit II is broken and reworked. The Steuben Expanded Stemmed point, variety small and thin, from Test Pit II is broken and partly reworked.

Hence, Snyders Corner Notched may belong in a Test Pit III context. Conversely, the Test Pit I assemblage at Steuben may include Marshall Barbed, variety fine; Steuben Expanded Stemmed, variety long and slender; and Contracting and Straight Stemmed, variety straight base. The Small Triangular-Shaped category, reminiscent of Maples Mills and Middle Mississippi forms, is represented by one specimen in Test Pit III. This projectile point was found in the plow zone and should be associated either with the latest Hopewell or with a post-Hopewell component at Steuben.

Other Flint Artifacts

Flint flakes are divisible into two major categories at Steuben: free flakes and ribbon flakes. Ribbon flakes, or blades, are long, thin, and slender parallel-sided, rectangular-shaped flakes which have been struck from specially prepared cores. Their major use was as knives with little or no further modification of the artifact being necessary. The free flake category includes nonparallel-sided flakes removed in the process of manufacturing a core, usually with some cortex exhibited on the outer surface; flakes removed to prepare a striking platform on a core; flakes to be made into projectile points, scrapers, and other flint artifacts; and trim flakes, produced during the process of trimming bifaced artifacts and consequently exhibiting at their bulbous end the edge of the artifacts being trimmed.

From one-fourth to over one-half of the flakes found in the excavation units at Steuben were utilized in some way (Table VIII). All of the blades or ribbon flakes seem to have been used, although at times it is difficult to determine whether flake scars on these artifacts are a result of natural causes as, for instance, frost action or accidental contact in, or outside of, the collection bags. For a description of the flint categories used in Table VIII, see the section entitled "Morse and UMMA Surface Collections from the Village," pp. 47-67. The Triangular Knife from Test Pit II is broken and unfinished. The Ribbon Flake with a Concave Edge from Test Pit III has four concavities on one edge and two on the other, each one-eighth of an inch wide. Three of the four concavities on the one edge of the artifact have flake scars showing its probable function as a spokeshave or as a sort of

TABLE VIII

FLINT ARTIFACTS FROM THE VILLAGE EXCAVATIONS AT THE STEUBEN SITE

Flint Category	Test Pit I						Test Pit II					Test Pit II Extension				Test Pit III			Test Pit III Extension	Total
	Levels						Levels					Levels				Levels			Level	
	1	2	3	4	5	6	1	2	4	5	6	1	2	3	F1	1	2	3	Upper	
Unused Free Flakes.	4	9	13	12	4	5	43	4	22	2	1	11	10	4	8	51	21	4	11	239
Free Flake Scraper, variety used	-	-	3	6	4	4	21	3	10	1	1	5	4	4	6	34	9	1	7	123
Free Flake Scraper, variety slightly worked	-	-	-	-	-	-	-	-	2	-	-	2	3	-	-	18	3	-	1	29
Free Flake Scraper, variety worked on all edges	-	-	1	-	-	-	-	-	-	-	-	-	1	-	1	-	-	-	-	3
Free Flake Scraper with concave edge	-	1	-	-	-	-	-	-	1	-	-	-	-	-	-	5	-	-	1	8
Free Flake End Scraper.	-	-	-	-	-	-	-	-	-	-	-	-	-	-	-	2	2	-	1	5
Ribbon Flake Knife, variety used	1	1	1	-	-	1	3	-	3	1	4	-	1	1	-	21	7	1	-	46
Ribbon Flake Knife, variety worked on one edge.	1	-	-	-	-	-	1	-	-	-	-	-	-	-	-	3	1	2	-	8
Ribbon Flake Knife, variety worked on both edges	-	-	-	1	-	-	-	-	1	-	-	-	1	-	-	4	2	1	-	10
Ribbon Flake Scraper with concave edge	-	-	-	-	-	-	-	-	-	-	-	-	-	-	-	-	-	1	-	1
Triangular Knife	1	-	-	-	-	-	-	1	-	-	-	-	-	-	-	-	-	-	-	2
Plano-Convex Scraper	-	-	-	-	-	-	-	-	-	-	-	-	-	-	-	-	-	-	1	1
Bifaced Scraper.	-	-	-	-	-	-	-	-	1	-	-	-	-	-	-	1	-	-	1	3
Graver made on Free Flake. .	-	-	-	-	-	-	-	-	-	-	-	-	-	-	-	1	-	-	-	1
Flint Hammerstone and/or Core.	-	2	-	1	1	1	14	-	2	-	-	4	-	1	-	2	-	-	2	30
Small Unworked Flint Nodule .	-	-	-	-	-	-	1	-	-	-	-	-	-	-	-	2	-	-	-	3
Total.	7	13	18	20	9	11	83	8	42	4	6	22	20	10	15	144	45	10	25	512

scarifier on wood or bone. The other concavities do not exhibit either use or retouch flake scars other than the initial breakage resulting in the concavities themselves. Since there is a greater amount of flint in Test Pit III in comparison to Test Pit I, it is to be expected that, correspondingly, there will be a greater variety in flint classes in Test Pit III. This is the case, especially within the free flake category.

While blades per se are not by any means restricted to Hopewell in the Eastern United States, it seems that the pyramidal and tongue core types are at least essentially Hopewell. In Illinois, blades used in post-Hopewellian times, with the exception of accidental occurrences which are actually by-products of a flaking technique, do not appear to constitute a tradition or industry until around Early Old Village times when there is present at Cahokia distinctive corner blades made from blocked-out flakes much in the manner of a burin flaking technique (Perino, 1960). These blades at Cahokia were then made into distinctive unifaced microdrills. At Cahokia, this industrial assemblage seems to represent a later independent development of blade production and seems to have been almost entirely confined to the Cahokia area, though they have been reported from other parts of the eastern United States as well (Lewis and Kneberg, 1956:117).

It is therefore reasonable to expect a significant difference in the number of blades between the two Late Hopewell components at Steuben. A significant difference is present, at a level of probability of around 0.01. The assemblage in Test Pit I has fewer blades in relation to all other flint than that in Test Pit III. This difference is another important indication of both the separation of the two test pit assemblages and the relative lateness of the Test Pit I assemblage.

Other Stone Artifacts

Small waterworn hematite and limonite fragments were fairly common throughout the various levels of the site. They are locally obtainable since inferior grades of hematite and limonite occur naturally in the soil. Hammerstones also were common in all the excavation units, there being eleven from Test Pit I, equally distributed as to depth below the ground surface. Occasionally, stone chips from the use of hammerstones were present in the excavations. A grooved abrader of sandstone was recovered from the general area of the burial in the extension of Test Pit III.

Copper Artifacts

Only one copper artifact was found in the village excavations at Steuben. It came from the 2.0-2.5-foot level of Test Pit II (Fig. 4). A total of eleven perforations are present on the cylindrical specimen, one of which may be natural. Nine of the other ten perforations are in each of the four corners of the rolled-up sheet and are either one-sixteenth or one-thirty-second of an inch in diameter. The other perforation is three-sixteenths of an inch in diameter and is in the center of the sheet near one end. The sheet (Fig. 4-C) measures two-and-seven-sixteenths of an inch long and one-and-one-sixteenths of an inch wide. At the two ends is an area about one-eighth of an inch wide which was folded beneath the sheet before the cylinder was formed. The cylinder measures two-and-three-sixteenths of an inch long and three-eighths of an inch in diameter. This cylindrical shape has been slightly distorted through flattening, as if it had been stepped upon.

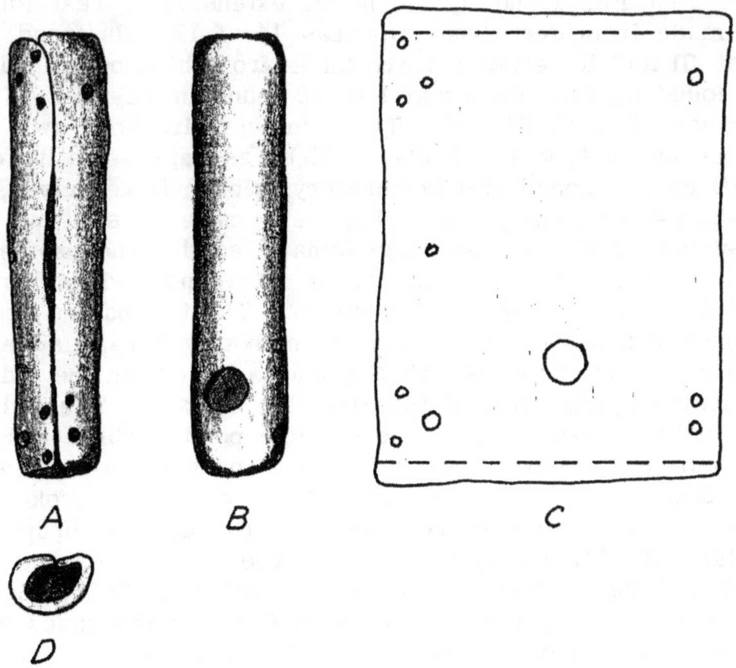

Fig. 4. Copper cylinder from Test Pit II, level 2.0-2.5'. A—reverse view. B—obverse view. C—cylinder unrolled. D—end view.

This artifact could have served as part of a whistle or even as the decorative end of a shaft, perhaps with the largest hole having been used for the insertion of a pearl. Its function remains obscure since there is nothing else reported quite like it.

Bone Awls

Bone awls, like many other artifact classes, have not been emphasized in site reports. Therefore, a comparison between Steuben and other awl assemblages is difficult. A general indication, however, is that the raw material for making awls is more limited at Steuben than at most other Hopewell sites. A total of 31 complete and fragmentary bone awls was found in the excavation units at Steuben. Table IX, modified from Kidder (1932:202), shows the provenience of the various kinds of awls.

It is at once apparent that there is a significant difference in awl categories between the two excavation areas. Of the 14 awls found in Test Pits I and II, and in the extension of Test Pit II, 13 are made from deer bone, whereas 14 of 17 awls found in Test Pit III and its extension are made from bird bone. Five of 6 awls found in Test Pit I and 1 of 10 found in Test Pit III are of deer bone (Pl. V, Fig. 1). The complete bird bone awls seem to cluster into a type which may well be as representative of Hopewell as are zoned-stamped pottery, ribbon-flake knives, and curved-based platform pipes. They were made by splitting the tarsometatarsus of a turkey longitudinally so that the proximal articular surface on either side of the intercondyloid eminence was retained by each of the two halves. The two halves are easily recognized and awls were made from both. The awls were finished by fairly complete grinding and polishing on the sides up to and including the rims of the articular surface. The finished awl gradually tapers to a fine needle-like point. Three-and-one-half to four-and-one-half inches seems to be the usual range in length. Sometimes part of the articular surface was broken off during splitting and occasionally an awl will have an abrupt point.

Mills (1909:44) describes this awl type as the sole one found in the Seip Mound. The two pictured by Mills (1909:36, Fig. 23) indicate that more care was taken with finishing the bases of these awls. Both have identically beveled heads which look somewhat like mushrooms.

This Hopewell type differs strikingly from awls made from identical bones in Fort Ancient and Indian Knoll complexes. In Fort Ancient, they are abundant and according to Mills (1922:110):

" . . . in practically every village site of this culture the awl made from this bone is present and very frequently exceed in numbers all other classes of awls." Griffin (1943:95), in describing the traits of the Anderson Focus, states that: "The most common awl was made from the metatarsal or the tibiotarsal bone of the wild turkey; such awls are 8.5 to 13 cm. long. The head or proximal part of the bone is usually unmodified, whereas the distal articulation is removed and that end of the shaft is sharpened. A few of these awls have distinctive transverse notches." From illustrations provided in Griffin and Mills, it seems that the sharpening of the Fort Ancient awls is usually lateral to the normal axis of the bone and that the cut for the awl point is usually about one-half the length of the awl.

At the Indian Knoll site (Oh-2) bird bone awls were abundant and "wild turkey bones seem to be the most widely used bird bones for awl manufacture" (Webb, 1946:284). Two awls in the University of Michigan Museum of Anthropology collection from the Read Shell Midden (Bt-10; Webb, 1950) are cut laterally, both for less than one-third of their length, and show but little modification of the proximal ends.

Undoubtedly, many more examples can be found to show greater details in differences of manufacture and thus the possibility of more types. It is sufficient to note here that numerous examples of the split turkey tarsometatarsus type are present in Illinois Hopewell in log tombs and in village collections. They are present in the Illinois Valley at least as early as the so-called Ogden-Fettie focus, around the time of the birth of Christ or a little earlier, along with the characteristic ten- to twelve-inch split elk long bone mat pins. At Steuben, the relative rarity of this awl type in the Test Pit I assemblage indicates that it was lost as an artifact type during, or immediately after, Late Hopewell in the Illinois Valley. At the least, another artifact type demonstrates a difference between Test Pits I and III, and the indication is again that Test Pit I is the latest of the two.

Bone Punctators

A total of five of these artifacts was found at Steuben, of which four came from the excavation units. They are either rare at Hopewell sites or overlooked for I could find mention of only one in the literature and this was from the Irving site (McGregor, 1958:147, and Fig. 50A, p. 148). As the name of the artifact class implies, there is good reason to infer that the function of

TABLE IX

BONE AWLS FROM THE VILLAGE EXCAVATIONS AT THE STEUBEN SITE

The awl categories are modified from Kidder (1932:202).

Awl Category	Test Pit I			Test Pit II			Test Pit II Extension	Test Pit III			Test Pit III Extension	Total
	Levels			Levels			Level	Levels			Level	
	3	5	6	1	3	4	4	1	2	3	1	
Deer metatarsal splinter, single-pointed.	1	1	-	1	1	-	-	-	-	-	-	4
Deer metatarsal splinter, double-pointed	-	-	1	-	-	1	-	-	-	-	-	2
Unclassifiable deer metatarsal	-	-	-	3	-	1	1	-	-	-	-	5
Unclassifiable deer ulna.	-	-	-	-	-	-	-	-	-	1	2	3
Unclassifiable mammal long bone . . .	2	-	-	-	-	-	-	-	-	-	-	2
Turkey tarsometatarsus split longitudinally	-	-	-	-	-	-	-	2	1	-	4	7
Unclassifiable bird long bone	-	1	-	-	-	-	-	-	6	-	1	8
Total	3	2	1	4	1	2	1	2	7	1	7	31

this artifact was to punctate pottery (Pl. V, Fig. 2). At Steuben, all five can be impressed into clay and the results compared favorably with Steuben Punctated sherds. A group of seven of these artifacts in the University of Michigan Museum of Anthropology was found with Burial 16 in Mound 16 at the Knight site. They were excavated by Mr. Walter Wadlow and presented to the Museum by Dr. P. F. Titterington. These specimens, while not producing good Steuben Punctates, do excellent Montezuma Punctates. In addition, they can be used to duplicate the zoning found on Havana Zoned Stamped vessels. The exact temporal placement of the Irving and Knight specimens is not known. The Irving specimen unfortunately was included in the general site collection. Burial 5 in Mound 16 at Knight had in association a Havana Zoned Dentate vessel. But the mounds seem to have late mantles added to the much earlier primary structures, and the relative position of Burial 5 is not known.

Table X shows that the artifacts from Steuben are usually made from the left ulna of a swan. The punctators are all well polished, especially at the distal end where the bone was cut. The beveled cut on the specimens from Test Pits I and III are polished to the extent that all signs of grinding marks have been obliterated. Both of these and the surface find are from ulnas which are smaller in diameter than the two from Test Pit II. The beveled cuts on the Steuben punctators range from about one-third to three-fourths of an inch in length, and the complete specimens, which have unmodified heads, range from six and one-fourth to ten inches in length. The beveled points are less abrupt on four of the five finished specimens from Knight, and the distal ends are more rounded than the ends of the Steuben punctators which approach being pointed. In the manufacture of the Knight specimens, both ends were either cut or broken off. At Steuben, these punctators may well belong in a Test Pit III assemblage since their occurrence elsewhere is with artifacts which reflect a mixture of the two Hopewell assemblages.

Game Bones

Two game bones are from the Steuben site; one was found in Level III and another in Level IV in Test Pit I (Pl. XII, Fig. 1). "Game bones" are worked deer phalanges. The distal end is notched[1] and the proximal end cut off so as to have a perforation

[1]Several similar artifacts found by my father and me at the Crable Site, a strong Middle Mississippi component site in Fulton County, Illinois, are, in general, drilled rather than notched at the distal end (Morse, 1959).

TABLE X

PROVENIENCE AND ZOOLOGICAL IDENTIFICATION OF THE BONE PUNCTATORS FROM THE STEUBEN VILLAGE SITE

Archaeological Unit	Level	Bone	Name	Species	Identifier
Surface.	-	Left ulna	Swan	*Cygnus sp.*	Philip Humphrey, University of Michigan
Test Pit I	3.0–3.5′	Left ulna	Swan	*Cygnus sp.*	Philip Humphrey, University of Michigan
Test Pit II	0.5–1.0′	Left ulna	Swan	*Cygnus sp.*	Peter Stettenheim, University of Michigan
Test Pit II	2.0–2.5′	Left ulna	Whistling swan	*Cygnus columbianus*	Peter Stettenheim, University of Michigan
Test Pit III.	1.0–1.5′	Left ulna	Size comparable to such birds as large hawk, great and blue heron, large gull, or goose.		Peter Stettenheim, University of Michigan

lengthwise through the phalange via the marrow cavity. The term "game bone" is used because of the similarity to artifacts used by many North American Indians in a sort of gambling game: "In the . . . game the ring or target is attached to a thong or cord by means of which it is swung in the air; the object being to catch it upon a pin or dart fastened to the other end of the thong. It is analogous to the well-known European game of cup and ball. . . . In point of fact, the targets are of the greatest possible variety, both in form and material, ranging from a single hide ring around the Tewa (Hano) to strings of imbricated phalangeal bones (Algonquian, Athapascan, and Siouan tribes). . . ." (Culin, 1907:527-28).

Other possible uses of such artifacts might have been as tinkling cones or beads. I know of none, however, which have been reported as having been found in association with a burial in such a way as to suggest an ornamental use. The ring and pin game, consisting of deer phalanges as rings or targets, had a wide distribution in historic times (Culin, 1907:527-61). This would indicate a respectable antiquity in North America—an inference which seems to be supported by archaeology if these artifacts described above were, in fact, targets in the ring and pin game. They occur in sites which are just prehistoric or earlier (Willoughby, 1935:217, 226-27; Barrett, 1933:527, 228, and 291), in Hopewell sites (Fowler, 1952:162, Plate Ln; and McGregor, 1958: Fig. 46, A-C), and even in Archaic deposits (Webb, 1946: 291). The Hopewell and Archaic occurrences are at multicomponent sites and thus could conceivably be post-Hopewell. Since none were present in Test Pit III at Steuben, perhaps this is another difference between the two Steuben Hopewell assemblages.

Turtle Carapace Artifacts

A total of 49 fragments of turtle shell vessels and/or spoons were found scattered throughout all levels of the site. Test Pit II produced 34 fragments, 12 of which were in level 1, and 13 in level 3. None constituted a complete specimen. Also, as in describing pottery fragments, pieces fitting together were counted as one. Fragments of turtle carapace artifacts can be recognized by unnatural striations on the inside of the shell as a result of cleaning and smoothing; from ground-down tubercles on the interior surface; and by the ground-down and polished rim areas. Worked turtle carapaces are very common at Hopewell sites and apparently are present at many pre- and post-Hopewell villages.

Drilled Bear Canines

A cache of four drilled, black bear canines was found in the 1.5-2.0-foot level at the center of Test Pit III. They were distributed in a six-inch vertical and horizontal area. Each canine had two perforations which were manufactured by drilling from both sides. There is no incised decoration and a depression for the reception of a pearl was not present on any of the canines. This latter attribute, however, is associated with pendants made from the larger grizzly bear canines.

Worked bear canines are common in Illinois Valley Hopewell, but the published descriptions are too vague to attempt a comparison of differences in manufacture to establish specific types. Considerable variation in details does exist and such a survey should prove fruitful. A comparison with specimens present in the collections at UMMA shows some of the range of variation. Three bone copies of bear canines are in the Museum of Anthropology from Burial 16, Mound 16, at the Knight site. Each has three perforations which were drilled completely through the specimen. One is presumably for attachment to the person and the other two, clustered together and apart from the first, for the attachment of some additional ornament. This may indicate why there were two holes in the Steuben specimens, and why they were drilled completely through the teeth. One perforation in the Steuben bear teeth was probably used for attachment to the clothing, and the other used to hold some other decorative affair. It is also possible that the Steuben canines were so drilled to enable them to be strung longitudinally. Four specimens found in Mound 1 at the Steuben site had two perforations apiece which penetrated only to the central cavity of the tooth, indicating attachment to a person's dress without additional attached decoration.

Other Bone Artifacts

Two worked-bone splinters were found. Both probably are split deer long bones and are either chisels or end scrapers. One is five and one-half inches long and three-fourths of an inch wide. It is from level 4, Test Pit II, and has been used at one end to the extent of being slightly polished and exhibiting scars where flakes were removed by use. The other splinter, from level 1, Test Pit II, is broken. It is one and one-half inches long and highly polished over most of its surface. The used end of the latter splinter shows considerably more polish than that of the former and, in addition, has been burned after having been broken.

Level 2 in the extension of Test Pit II produced a deer ulna which seems to have been used as a chisel or a scraper. A bone chip, probably from a deer long bone, was found in Level 3, Test Pit II. This chip is irregular in shape and its dimensions are one by one-half by one-fourth inches. This specimen is unusual because it is completely smoothed and polished as if carried around for a long period of time. There are no signs of deliberate polishing; that is, there are no striations present on the bone chip. Its function is unknown.

A total of six small fragments of bone tools are unidentifiable. All seem to be portions of artifacts made from deer bone. Many or possibly all may be awl fragments.

Barbed Antler Tines

Only one artifact is represented for this category and it is unfinished. This specimen was found beneath Burial 3 in the extension of Test Pit III. Polishing to the extent of obliterating the rough surface at the tip and base, a general over-all polish, and a battered tip indicate that the original function may have been as a flaking implement. There are good indications, however, that its intended function was to be an atlatl hook. The base of the antler tine exhibits evidence that it was detached from a deer rack by at least two blows from an axe, probably a hafted stone celt. The artifact is five and one-half inches long and about three-fourths of an inch in diameter at the base. Two incisions are present; one three inches and one three and one-half inches from the tip. These incisions are deep, about half way through to the spongy interior, and indicate that the roughed-out blank would have had the characteristic 45 degree bevel that is found on many barbed antler tines.

Several specimens from the Snyders and Knight sites in the Museum of Anthropology show the steps of manufacture. After the blank was detached, the spongy interior was removed and the artifact was cut and ground much like the flat-based Indian Knoll antler projectile points which have been found embedded in human vertebrae (Moore, 1916:478, Fig. 20; Webb and Haag, 1940:91, Fig. 16). The natural antler curve below the barb was straightened by the cutting and grinding process. The bases were finished in much the same way. The barb was ground, probably with a flat sandstone abrader, but only slightly, thus leaving remnants of the original cut and a slight beveling effect which accentuated the point of the barb. The remainder of the base was cut and ground until almost perpendicular to the longitudinal axis of the artifact, with the lip either beveled inward or ground straight. This latter process caused the barb to be even more prominent.

As far as I have been able to find out, these artifacts are called projectile points. I suggest, rather, that their function was that of atlatl hooks. Several reasons for this interpretation can be pointed out. There is ample evidence of the atlatl being present in Hopewell (Kellar, 1955:319; Deuel, 1952, Fig. 84A; McKern, Titterington, and Griffin, 1945, Plate XX). Also, the careful preparation of the barb is noteworthy. The barb always curved outward, and all the blanks examined had been cut so as to have the barb on the concave side of the antler; that is, where the antler curved outward from the main axis. The barbs do project far enough to effectively function as atlatl hooks. It would take considerable use as an atlatl hook to polish the tip, and several specimens exhibit this polish. Specimens which do not exhibit this polishing effect were apparently unfinished, split, or broken during, or soon after, their manufacture, or were not used enough.[2]

Three unfinished specimens associated with Burial 9, Mound 3, at the Knight site are in the University of Michigan Museum of Anthropology. One exhibits only the axe blows at the base. The other two were cut, one probably with a sandstone saw and the other with a flint knife, and broken off at the cut ends. On both of the pointed tips, hooks were being cut out which were similar to the Indian Knoll specimens pictured in Moore (1916: 455, Fig. 10-D). On both of the Knight artifacts, a beginning had been made to gouge out the spongy interior for attachment. The finished specimens would have been around four inches in length if the barbs were retained.

A similar artifact from square 0-0, level 2 (6-12 inches below the surface), of the Museum of Anthropology's excavations at the Snyders site appears finished, but, though a barb is present, there is no real point. Instead, this end curves upward in the Indian Knoll style, and there are cutting marks present which

[2]I should like to thank Mr. D. Barney Cochran, a graduate student in anthropology at The University of Michigan, for some very helpful hints concerning whether these specimens may have served as atlatl hooks. Mr. Cochran has had much experience in manufacturing and using atlatls, and it is his opinion that these barbed, antler tine artifacts could have served effectively as atlatl hooks.

indicate either an attempt to fashion a hook at the end or to cut off this part. Since the cuts are all at the same locus, however, and not completely around the artifact, it is doubtful that the end was about to be cut off. In addition, the specimen seems to have been cut so as to elevate this area even more. An atlatl hook similar in form to the Snyders artifact is pictured in Moore (1916:455, Fig. 10-B).

Three very interesting tine artifacts were found in Mound 6 at the Havana site (Baker, and others, 1941, Pl. 6, Figs. 1 and 4). Shown in their Figure 1 is a typical example of a discarded cut antler fragment from which a barbed antler blank for an atlatl hook has been detached. In their Figure 4 are two barbed antler specimens. Both lack sockets for attachment, and unless a sort of wrap-around staff was used, it seems reasonable to expect that they are broken at the bases.[3]

Two artifacts like those being discussed in this section were found at Lu°61 (Webb and DeJarnette, 1942, Pl. 166-1, upper left-hand corner). Interestingly, some of the associated flint and pottery is similar to Hopewell (*ibid.*, Pls. 165, 167). In the Pickwick Basin at sites Lu°25, Unit 1, and at Lu°92, barbed antler artifacts seem to be associated only with Moundville-like complexes (*ibid.*, Pls. 120-22). The pointed ends appear sharp and they may be a sort of toggle-head harpoon point. The atlatl, however, in the Southeast lasted into historic times (Kellar, 1955:321), thus the function of the Pickwick specimens is not certainly known. But the historic atlatls apparently were not composite in form as were the Indian Knoll specimens.

There do not seem to be any common artifacts which might have served as weights or handles in Hopewell. If these barbed antler artifacts are atlatl hooks, then it is noteworthy that the small notched and unnotched triangular projectile points may first appear about the latter part of Late Hopewell at Steuben and at other sites. None, however, have been definitely associated with Hopewell. Whether the rarity of the antler artifacts at Steuben in addition to the presence of these small flint projectile points can be inferred to indicate that the bow and arrow was just successfully replacing the atlatl as the major weapon at this time is a tantalizing hypothesis.

[3]Elaine Bluhm, secretary for the Illinois Archaeological Survey, wrote to me that, although one may be broken, the other doesn't seem to be. Both are described as in a chalky condition, however, and thus not very well preserved. Hence, it is difficult to determine exactly their original basal form.

Other Antler Artifacts

As far as can be ascertained, the remaining artifacts of antler could have been meant for one or another of four functions: (1) as a handle for such items as copper punches or awls; (2) as a hafted or unhafted pressure-flaking tool; (3) as a barbed or unbarbed projectile point or atlatl hook; and (4) as a punch or awl. Some or many may be unfinished.

All of the antler tines have been ground or polished at the tip or over the whole artifact. Most show evidence of hacking scars at the base. Almost half of them have had the spongy bone cleaned from the base, but only one, and possibly another, exhibits any evidence of having been drilled at the base. However, evidence of drilling is hard to demonstrate on the Steuben artifacts since the spongy bone is, in general, very fragile. Most of the specimens show scars on the tip which perhaps may be interpreted as resulting from use in pressure-flaking flint.

Seven such artifacts were found: Test Pit I contained one in the 2.0-2.5-foot level; the extension of Test Pit II contained two in the 1.5-2.5-foot level; one was in the Burial level of the extension of Test Pit III; and three were found in Test Pit III, ranging in depth from 0.5 to 2.0 feet below the surface. A total of eight antler fragments of indeterminable function were found; four were distributed from the surface to 2.0 feet below the surface of Test Pit III; one was in the 1.5-2.0-foot level of Test Pit II; and three were found in the 2.0-2.5-foot level of the extension of Test Pit II. This gives a total of seven in Test Pit III as against one for Test Pit I. But it is difficult to determine how significant this large difference in proportion really is.

Shell Hoes

Shell hoes are fairly common at Hopewell and post-Hopewell sites (Pl. VI, Fig. 1). Mussel shells, usually *Megalonaias gigantea,* are perforated near the center of the valve with the perforation ranging from one-half to three-fourths of an inch in diameter. Rarely, the hinge is ground down. Many of these artifacts show chipped and polished bits.

A total of 22 shell hoes were found in most of the levels in the village site excavations. One of the hoes from level 1 of Test Pit III is unperforated but the hinge is ground down. The majority of the shell hoes were made from the right valves. The range in length varies between two and three-fourths and six inches for the majority of the specimens from Steuben.

Shell Scrapers

In Test Pit II, two possible shell scrapers were found; one is from level 1 and the other from level 3. Both are the left valves of mussel shells, *Amblema peruviana* and *Actinonaias carinata* respectively. The former is chipped from wear almost completely along the outer edge, and no other signs of use nor of any deliberate workmanship is present. The flake scars are all on the inside of the valve, indicating a single direction of motion. The other shell has only a few flake scars, again from use rather than from intentional chipping. These flake scars, however, are all on the exterior surface of the valve.

Other Shell Artifacts

No recognizable shell spoons were collected in the excavation units. The only other type of shell artifact consisted of two specimens from the 1.5-2.0-foot level of Test Pit II, and the 1.0-1.5-foot level of Test Pit III, respectively. Both a left and a right valve of *Actinonaias carinata* are represented, each of which is perforated slightly off center. The perforation in each case is slightly oval and about one-fourth of an inch long. The exterior surface of the specimen from Test Pit II has been ground down an eighth of an inch over the area containing the perforation resulting in a sort of fluting effect oriented with the hole and the valve. These shell artifacts are probably rattles.

MORSE AND UMMA SURFACE COLLECTIONS FROM THE VILLAGE

The majority of the material represented in this section was collected from the surface of the site. The rest was collected while digging various small test pits. The collections include material found by Dr. Dan Morse and myself between 1949 and 1957, and by the Museum of Anthropology (UMMA) in the spring of 1956. Most of the specimens found by Mr. George Schoenbeck between 1951 and just before his death in the winter of 1955 are included in the Morse collection.

Pottery

A total of 1,550 sherds was collected from the village, of which 478 were found by the Museum of Anthropology in 1956 (Table XI). The Morse collection is not a random sample because of our collecting habits during the first few years of obtaining surface material. It may be assumed that the Museum of Anthropology collection is one of the most random from the site, since all recognized artifacts on the ground surface were picked up. Over the years, the amount of influence the presence of other collectors on the site might have had on the randomness of the UMMA sample is of course unknown. The site had just been planted in wheat and was in excellent condition for surface hunting.

There is not a significant difference between a comparison of Test Pits I and III combined and Test Pit II and its extension, including Feature 4, combined: a chi-square test showed a level of probability of greater than 0.40. But there is a significant difference, a level of probability of less than 0.001, between all test pits combined as compared with the UMMA surface collection on the level of comparison of wares. Two possible explanations are readily apparent assuming: (1) that the UMMA collection is as random as possible considering the circumstances; and (2) that the combined test pits represent an equal combination of the two components. One explanation is that one component occupied the site longer than the other. The second possible explanation is that the collection is not random over the whole site. In fact, a large part of the western side is not under cultivation. Hence, the indication is that one of the components is not equally represented in the surface collection. The surface collection contains more Havana ware than Weaver ware, whereas the reverse is true of the test pit combination (Table XII). In addition, the surface collection contains more Hopewell ware. This indicates that the Test Pit I assemblage is not equally represented in the surface collection.

Plain and Cordmarked Types.—A total of 11 Havana Cordmarked and 2 Havana Plain rim sherds is present in both collections. This reflects, perhaps, the general domination of cordmarked over plain in the basically Havana component represented by Test Pit III. Only 2 rims of each type, however, are represented in the Museum of Anthropology collection. Whereas a total of 19 Weaver Cordmarked and 14 Weaver Plain rim sherds is represented as a whole, only 2 of the plain sherds and none of the cordmarked specimens were found by the Museum.

TABLE XI

POTTERY FROM THE SURFACE OF THE STEUBEN VILLAGE SITE IN THE MORSE AND UMMA COLLECTIONS

Type	Morse Collection		UMMA Collection		Total
	Number	Per Cent	Number	Per Cent	
Havana Plain.	215	20.06	111	23.22	326
Havana Cordmarked. . . .	170	15.86	107	22.37	277
Steuben Punctated	167	15.58	33	6.90	200
Naples Dentate Stamped. .	67	6.25	9	1.88	76
Hummel Dentate Stamped.	52	4.85	5	1.05	57
Naples Barred Ovoid Stamped.	2	0.19	-	-	2
Neteler Dentate Crescent Stamped.	1	0.09	-	-	1
Havana Miscellaneous Incised	5	0.47	2	0.42	7
Victory Brushed	1	0.09	-	-	1
Havana Cross-hatched Rim	1	0.09	-	-	1
Total Havana	681	63.53	267	55.84	948
Weaver Plain	146	13.62	78	16.32	224
Weaver Cordmarked. . . .	165	15.39	111	23.22	276
Weaver Plain Stamped . .	8	0.75	-	-	8
Weaver Wavy or Notched Rim	7	0.65	2	0.42	9
Weaver Cord-wrapped Stick Stamped.	3	0.28	1	0.21	4
Weaver Incised	1	0.09	2	0.42	3
Weaver Other	-	-	1	0.21	1
Total Weaver. . . .	330	30.78	195	40.80	525
Hopewell Rim	7	0.65	1	0.21	8
Hopewell Zoned Rocked Dentate Stamped	14	1.31	2	0.42	16
Hopewell Zoned Incised. .	3	0.28	1	0.21	4
Hopewell Plain Rocked Stamped.	11	1.03	1	0.21	12
Hopewell Dentate Rocked Stamped.	3	0.28	1	0.21	4
Hopewell Plain	4	0.37	3	0.63	7
Brangenburg Plain.	-	-	1	0.21	1
Hopewell Zoned Red Filmed	-	-	1	0.21	1
Baehr Zoned Brushed . . .	1	0.09	-	-	1
Baehr Brushed	18	1.68	5	1.05	23
Total Hopewell. . .	61	5.69	16	3.36	77
Total sherds	1072	100.00	478	100.00	1550

TABLE XII

COMPARISON OF THE MUSEUM OF ANTHROPOLOGY SURFACE COLLECTION OF POTTERY WITH THE COMBINED VILLAGE EXCAVATION UNITS

Ware	Test Pit II, Its Extension, and Features		Test Pit III and Test Pit I		UMMA Surface Collection		Total
	Number	Per Cent	Number	Per Cent	Number	Per Cent	
Havana. . . .	680	44.68	458	45.98	267	55.84	1405
Weaver. . . .	802	52.69	519	52.11	195	40.80	1516
Hopewell. . .	40	2.63	19	1.91	16	3.36	75
Total. . .	1522	100.00	996	100.00	478	100.00	2996

Two rim sherds classified as Weaver Cordmarked exhibit exterior nodes; neither was found by the Museum group. Interestingly, a Havana Plain body sherd is shell-tempered. It is my understanding that one or two other similar specimens have been found on Hopewell sites in the Illinois Valley. Another Havana Plain rim sherd exhibits an exterior node which was appliqued rather than punched out from the interior surface.

Steuben Punctated (Pl. III, Fig. 2 and Pl. V, Fig. 2).—As might be expected, Steuben Punctated is the most numerous of the rim decorative types, since this is the type site. Generally, the vessel shape is typically Havana with fairly straight sides, slightly pointed bases, and a slight outflaring at the shoulders. There are six rim sherds, which to all appearances are from bowls, but this probably is due to the slight channeling found on jar rim sherds. The Steuben Punctated decoration is found superimposed over both plain and cordmarked exterior surfaces. But it is much more commonly found on plain sherds, the rim area probably having been smoothed over on most cordmarked vessels.

The majority of the Steuben punctates seem to have been made with a hollow cylindrical punch, for there is a slight raised area in the center of many of the punctates. A few sherds exhibit punctates made with either a bundle of twigs or the corner of a cord-wrapped paddle. Variations in the shapes of punctates are the following:

Cone-shaped	131
Semicircular, much like the letter D	27
Circular	31
Total	189

The number of rows of punctates also varies as follows:

One row	2
Two rows	75
Three rows	73
Four rows	2
Indeterminable	37
Total	189

Most commonly, as reflected by these figures, Steuben Punctated sherds have two to three rows of cone-shaped punctates just below the lip. While Weaver ware is noted, in general, for a rounded lip, the typical Havana lip is flat or sharply beveled. Thus, it is interesting to note that a sorting of 189 Steuben Punctated rim sherds results in the following:

Flat or sharply beveled	61
Rounded	40
Intermediate	78
Indeterminable	10
Total	189

Hence, though there is a slight tendency toward the typical Havana lip cross-section on Steuben Punctated sherds, most are intermediate between the typical Havana and Weaver shapes.

The 11 sherds not included in the preceding breakdowns have a paste which is very similar to Weaver. Most commonly, on these sherds, there is exhibited one horizontal row of small cone-shaped punctates just beneath a flattened lip. On some sherds, as many as three rows are present. These 11 specimens well may represent a Weaver type which grew out of Steuben Punctated, or they may be just a short-lived variation of Steuben Punctated.

Other Types.—Most of the remaining stamped Havana rim sherds are cordmarked. Eight of the dentate variety exhibit two to three square elements in each vertical row. The general rule is four to eight square elements, while one sherd contains as many as sixteen. Two unusual sherds are present in the surface collection (Pl. II, Fig. 2). One sherd exhibits alternating vertical rows of round and of square dentate elements. Another sherd has been treated with two horizontal series of overlapping Hummel Dentate Stamped motifs.

Two fragmentary pottery vessels were found in the western side of the village site mound into which Test Pit III was excavated. One is represented by 79 Havana Plain body sherds and three Steuben Punctated rim sherds, and the other consists of

27 Havana Cordmarked body sherds and two Hummel Dentate Stamped rim sherds. The Steuben Punctated vessel was stratigraphically above the other; however, they were not in the same test pit.

Havana Miscellaneous Incised is a category used here to include Havana sherds which have vertically or horizontally placed incised lines, usually on the upper rim area. The incisions are carelessly done, and in some cases seem to be closely related to Steuben Punctated and to Naples Stamped decorative treatments. The Victory Brushed sherd is a Steuben Punctated rim which also exhibits a coarse-brushed surface treatment.

Weaver Incised is a body treatment of Weaver sherds in which incised lines are arranged in some sort of geometric pattern (Pl. IV, Fig. 2). The body sherd in the Morse collection has a large crosshatched motif on it. Another body sherd exhibits parts of three curved lines, one of which could be part of a circle with the other two lines radiating from it. The third specimen is a notched rim with a horizontal incision just below the lip and part of an incised rectangle on the extreme upper shoulder. The nature of the incision is consistent on a given sherd, but varies between sherds as to whether it is broad, fine, shallow, or deep. The sherd classified as Weaver Other is a plain rim which has a shallow Hopewell-like channel but which is Weaver in paste.

The majority of the Hopewell ware sherds are limestone-tempered and the remainder are tempered with small crushed grit (Pl. IV, Fig. 2). About one-third of the decorated sherds exhibit a carelessness of application which is not usually found in such a high proportion in other Hopewell sites in the Illinois Valley. A Hopewell Zoned Red sherd is zoned incised but is unusual since the complete exterior surface, not just the zoned areas, is red filmed. One of the Hopewell Dentate Rocked Stamped sherds in the Morse collection has a T-shaped Brangenburg rim and is red filmed on the lip and the interior surface.

Projectile Points, Notched Scrapers, and Drills

This collection includes 209 classifiable projectile points, 152 of which are not damaged. An additional 76 specimens were rendered unclassifiable through breakage. In addition to the projectile points, there are 13 drills and 16 notched scrapers (Pl. VI, Fig. 2). The drills and notched scrapers are described with the projectile points because each can be placed into one of the projectile point categories. All of these artifacts are between one-half and five inches in length. To avoid any confusion which might arise as to the variability of each of my categories, each column in Table XIII shows the number of projectile points in each category which exhibits a particular trait. In addition, the photographs of the representative specimens show the variability within each of these divisions. The Steuben Expanded Stemmed and Marshall Barbed projectile point types derive their respective designations from Steuben Township, and Marshall County, but both names are purely locally used terms. They and the other projectile point, as well as the other flint category designations are utilized in place of the commonly used numerical or alphabetical symbols which are usually too complex to retain easily.

Snyders Corner Notched (Pl. VII, Fig. 1).—Eleven projectile points and 4 notched scrapers are represented. Typically, they are quite broad, corner notched, and have convex bases. The majority are between one and two and-one-half inches in length, being somewhat smaller than is usually the case with similar specimens found on other Hopewell Sites in the Illinois Valley. Workmanship is exceedingly fine, and it is inferred that great care was taken in their fabrication. An attempt had been made to convert one of the broken points into a knife or scraper, but this was prevented by the specimen breaking again. Another point has a worn or ground base, and one of the 11 points is unifaced. That is, this specimen was made from a flake which was not modified to the extent that the bifaced implement has an oval cross section. Though called an unifaced implement, this projectile point exhibits trim flakes on its reverse surface; however, these trim flakes do not obscure very much of the reverse surface of the original flake from which the point was made. This is the definition of "uniface" which is used in this paper.

Marshall Barbed (Pl. VII, Fig. 2).—In general, these 39 projectile points and 2 notched scrapers are very similar to Snyders Corner Notched, but do not have the characteristic squat appearance. In addition, the blade edges of Marshall Barbed are straighter than those of Snyders Corner Notched. This combination serves to set the two categories apart, though both are essentially corner notched projectile points. Snyders Corner Notched seems to be restricted mainly to Hopewellian times, while Marshall Barbed may range anywhere from Early Woodland times up into the Late Woodland period. Marshall Barbed is divided into three varieties: fine, rugged, and crude.

TABLE XIII

ATTRIBUTES OF PROJECTILE POINTS, MORSE, AND UMMA STEUBEN SURFACE COLLECTIONS

Type				Base					Notch/Stem				Stem (Notch) to Blade Ratio											
	Number	Per Cent of Total	Number Broken	Pointed	Convex	Straight	Concave	Unclassified	Stemmed	Corner	Side	Un-notched	1:1	1:1.5	1:2	1:2.5	1:3	1:3.5	1:4	1:4.5	1:5	1:6	1:7	Unclassified
Snyders Corner Notched.	11	5.3	5	-	11	-	-	-	-	11	-	-	-	-	-	2	1	-	1	-	5	1	1	-
Marshall Barbed, variety fine.	23	11.0	8	-	2	17	-	4	-	23	-	-	-	1	7	1	12	-	-	-	2	-	-	-
Marshall Barbed, variety rugged. . . .	7	3.4	3	-	6	1	-	-	-	7	-	-	-	-	-	-	2	1	3	-	1	-	-	-
Marshall Barbed, variety crude.	9	4.3	5	-	8	-	-	1	-	9	-	-	-	-	-	-	2	-	7	-	-	-	-	-
Steuben Expanded Stemmed, variety long and slender	25	12.0	6	-	-	20	5	-	-	25	-	-	-	-	4	5	13	1	2	-	-	-	-	-
Steuben Expanded Stemmed, variety squat and thick	13	6.2	4	-	6	7	-	-	-	13	-	-	1	-	1	2	4	3	2	-	-	-	-	-
Steuben Expanded Stemmed, variety small and thin.	14	6.7	1	-	10	1	3	-	-	14	-	-	10	-	4	-	-	-	-	-	-	-	-	-
Large Side Notched, variety straight and concave base	32	15.3	8	-	-	25	7	-	-	-	32	-	-	-	8	5	12	3	2	-	1	1	-	-
Large Side Notched, variety convex base.	32	15.3	9	-	32	-	-	-	-	-	32	-	-	-	1	1	6	-	10	2	7	1	4	-
Contracting and Straight Stemmed, variety pointed base	4	1.9	2	4	-	-	-	-	4	-	-	-	-	1	2	1	-	-	-	-	-	-	-	-
Contracting and Straight Stemmed, variety rounded base.	9	4.3	1	-	9	-	-	-	9	-	-	-	-	-	6	2	1	-	-	-	-	-	-	-
Contracting and Straight Stemmed, variety straight base.	17	8.1	3	-	-	17	-	-	17	-	-	-	-	-	2	3	8	1	1	-	1	1	-	-
Small Triangular.	13	6.2	2	-	4	7	1	1	-	3	8	2	-	-	-	-	-	-	1	-	2	2	6	2
Total	209	100.0	57	4	88	95	16	6	30	105	72	2	11	2	35	22	61	9	29	2	19	6	11	2

TABLE XIII (Continued)

Type	Shoulders					Length								Length to Width Ratio							Thick-ness			Cross Section	
	Number	Sloping	Straight	Barbed	Unclassified	.5"-1"	1"-1.5"	1.5"-2"	2"-2.5"	2.5"-3"	3"-3.5"	4"-4.5"	4.5"-5"	1:1	1.5:1	2:1	2.5:1	3:1	4:1	5:1	-1/8"	1/8"-1/4"	1/4"-1/2"	Planoconvex	Biconvex
Snyders Corner Notched	11	-	3	8	-	-	4	4	2	-	1	-	-	-	11	-	-	-	-	-	-	9	2	-	11
Marshall Barbed, variety fine	23	-	-	23	-	-	5	11	5	1	-	-	-	-	2	14	5	2	-	-	3	10	10	2	21
Marshall Barbed, variety rugged	7	-	-	7	-	-	-	1	3	3	-	-	-	-	1	6	-	-	-	-	-	-	7	2	5
Marshall Barbed, variety crude	9	-	-	9	-	-	2	7	-	-	-	-	-	-	5	2	-	2	-	-	-	3	6	1	8
Steuben Expanded Stemmed, variety long and slender	25	10	15	-	-	-	2	14	6	2	-	1	-	-	1	18	1	4	1	-	-	13	12	1	24
Steuben Expanded Stemmed, variety squat and thick	13	1	12	-	-	-	2	7	4	-	-	-	-	-	3	10	-	-	-	-	-	4	9	1	12
Steuben Expanded Stemmed, variety small and thin	14	11	3	-	-	-	14	-	-	-	-	-	-	-	6	8	-	-	-	-	-	4	10	-	14
Large Side Notched, variety straight and concave base	32	12	20	-	-	-	6	23	3	-	-	-	-	-	7	25	-	-	-	-	-	7	25	4	28
Large Side Notched, variety convex base	32	15	17	-	-	-	10	15	6	-	-	-	1	-	10	12	6	3	-	1	-	13	19	3	29
Contracting and Straight Stemmed, variety pointed base	4	1	3	-	-	-	-	1	3	-	-	-	-	-	-	-	4	-	-	-	-	4	-	1	3
Contracting and Straight Stemmed, variety rounded base	9	4	5	-	-	-	4	2	3	-	-	-	-	-	6	-	1	2	-	-	-	8	1	-	9
Contracting and Straight Stemmed, variety straight base	17	2	15	-	-	-	2	6	8	1	-	-	-	-	4	9	4	-	-	-	-	12	5	-	17
Small Triangular	13	2	9	-	2	3	10	-	-	-	-	-	-	1	1	11	-	-	-	-	13	-	-	-	13
Total	209	58	102	47	2	3	61	91	43	7	1	1	1	1	57	115	21	13	1	1	16	87	106	15	194

TABLE XIII (Continued)

Type	Number	Blade Edge			Color of Flint							
		Straight	Curved	Unclassified	White	Light Gray	Dark Gray	Brown	Black	Red	Pink	Multicolored
Snyders Corner Notched	11	-	11	-	2	2	1	1	1	-	-	4
Marshall Barbed, variety fine	23	5	18	-	3	5	2	2	2	1	1	7
Marshall Barbed, variety rugged	7	2	4	1	2	2	-	-	2	-	-	1
Marshall Barbed, variety crude	9	-	9	-	3	1	-	-	-	-	-	5
Steuben Expanded Stemmed, variety long and slender	25	3	19	3	7	4	6	3	-	1	1	4
Steuben Expanded Stemmed, variety squat and thick	13	1	12	-	6	3	1	1	-	1	-	-
Steuben Expanded Stemmed, variety small and thin	14	1	13	-	6	5	-	2	-	-	-	1
Large Side Notched, variety straight and concave base	32	6	26	-	2	9	2	-	1	3	7	8
Large Side Notched, variety convex base	32	5	27	-	12	1	5	2	1	1	4	6
Contracting and Straight Stemmed, variety pointed base	4	3	1	-	1	-	-	-	-	1	1	1
Contracting and Straight Stemmed, variety rounded base	9	3	6	-	4	-	-	1	-	-	-	4
Contracting and Straight Stemmed, variety straight base	17	5	9	3	10	-	2	-	1	2	2	2
Small Triangular	13	6	7	-	3	3	-	1	-	-	-	4
Total	209	40	162	7	61	35	19	13	8	10	16	47

Marshall Barbed, variety fine, is represented by 23 projectile points and two notched scrapers. All are between one and two and one-half inches in length, generally one and one-half to two inches. In general, the length-to-width ratio is 2-2.5:1, with a thickness of about one-fourth of an inch. The workmanship is fair to very fine. Two points are essentially unifacial, 3 have ground bases, and another's blade has been reworked.

Seven points are larger, two to three inches long, and thicker, about one-half of an inch. These make up the rugged variety of Marshall Barbed. The length-to-width ratio is 2:1, workmanship is fair to good, and one point has a ground base.

The nine projectile points included in Marshall Barbed, variety crude, exhibit very poor care in manufacture. Generally broader than the other two varieties, they range around one and one-half inches in length, and none are longer than two inches. Bases are about one-half as wide as the blades, some being not much wider than the stems.

Steuben Expanded Stemmed (Pl. VIII, Fig. 1).—Those corner notched points which exhibit straight or sloping shoulders form this category. They seem quite different from the Archaic expanding stemmed points and may be confined in time to around Late Hopewell. There are three varieties: long and slender, squat and thick, and small and thin.

Steuben Expanded Stemmed, variety long and slender, is the largest subgroup and consists of 25 projectile points, 4 notched scrapers, and 4 drills. Apparently this was the most popular variety since there seems to be a considerable variation in functions. The specimens are all fairly slender, with a 2-3:1 length-to-width ratio, and they have long stems which expand gently to straight and concave bases. The majority are fairly thin in proportion to their length and width, with the exception of 2 scrapers and 1 projectile point. Length is fairly consistent at about two inches with the exception of 3 drills, one inch long, and a projectile point four and one-quarter inches long. Workmanship is fine, and one of the points exhibits a ground base.

Steuben Expanded Stemmed, variety squat and thick, on the average, is shorter, broader, thicker, and exhibits cruder workmanship than variety long and slender. This, in addition to the absence of scrapers and drills indicates a distinctive function for the 13 included projectile points. The 14 points included in Steuben Expanded Stemmed, variety small and thin, might also have been made for a specific use. Certainly, this variety is a very compact category. The projectile points are quite small, one to one and one-half inches in length, broad, and strikingly similar in shape with the exception of basal construction. They are also interesting because of the type of notch, which appears intermediate between a side and a corner notch, and which causes this variety to be similar to Large Side Notched, variety straight and concave base.

Large Side Notched (Pl. VIII, Fig. 2).—All of the large side-notched points found at Steuben are included in this category. The breakdown into varieties of the 64 points, 5 drills, and 4 notched scrapers first resulted in 6 subgroups which since have been combined into 2. This change reflects the general difficulty in segregating and defining varieties for the Large Side Notched type.

Large Side Notched, variety straight and concave base, is represented by 32 projectile points and three notched scrapers. In general, they have a 2-3:1 notch to blade ratio, and a 2:1 length-to-width ratio. All have straight or slightly concave bases, and workmanship is crude to good. Two points are unifaced, 5 have a ground base, and 2 exhibit reworked blades. One of the notched scrapers approaches the so-called "Black Sand" type (also called Hemphill or Osceola), a side-notched narrow point with a concave base. This type seems to have been prominent around Late Archaic, probably "Transitional Archaic" times, possibly lasting into the Early Woodland period (Morse, 1959).

A total of 32 points, 4 drills, and 1 notched scraper make up Large Side Notched, variety convex base. The majority have a length-to-width ratio of 1.5-2.5:1, and a notch-to-blade ratio of 3-6:1. Workmanship is usually good to very good while a few specimens are very finely made. All of the specimens included in this subgroup have convex bases. Two projectile points are unifaced, and 2 others have ground bases.

Contracting and Straight Stemmed (Pl. VII, Fig. 1).—A total of 30 projectile points, 2 notched scrapers, and 2 drills are divided into 3 varieties according to their basal construction: (1) pointed, (2) rounded, and (3) straight. Straight stemmed points were present in Red Ocher in central Illinois (Morse, 1959), but those at Steuben may be actually variations of the Steuben Expanded Stemmed category. Rounded and pointed stemmed projectile points similar to those found at Steuben may range anywhere between Late Archaic times through the Middle Hopewellian period.

The smallest group, Contracting and Straight Stemmed, variety pointed base, is represented by 4 projectile points and 2 drills. Both drills exhibit ground or worn blades and stems. All

6 specimens are about two to two and one-half inches in length, are quite narrow, with the exception of 1 projectile point; are fairly thin; and are of good to fine workmanship. The stem is generally one half as long as the complete specimen. In addition, the base is constructed much like a triangle which is balanced very nicely with a similarly shaped blade. One projectile point is unifaced.

Nine projectile points and 1 scraper make up the rounded base variety of Contracting and Straight Stemmed. Generally broader and a little more crudely made than the pointed variety, the bases are rounded off before the apex of a triangle would have been reached. The blade-to-stem ratio, however, is still about 2:1. Five projectile points are about the same length as those in the pointed variety, while the remaining 4 are approximately an inch shorter; the scraper is a little over 2 inches long. Two projectile points have worn bases and another's base has been reworked.

A total of 17 points and 1 notched scraper exhibit straight bases and stems, thus making up the third variety of Contracting and Straight Stemmed. They are very close in appearance to the members of the pointed base variety. Specimens of the straight base variety are about one and one-half to two and one-half inches in length, are fairly narrow, have a 3:1 stem-to-blade ratio, and are of good workmanship. One of the projectile points has a ground base, and another a reworked base.

Small Triangular (Pl. VII, Fig. 1).—The 13 points and 2 drills which make up this category are very similar to those specimens commonly found on Late Woodland and Middle Mississippi sites. But, unlike the majority of Mississippi points though more in accord with Late Woodland forms, only 1 is a unifacial specimen. In addition, only 2 are unnotched, but these specimens are probably unfinished since each exhibits a hump on the blade back. Projectile points belonging to this category were numerous around Maples Mills and Mississippi times. The drills, which are described here because they are closest to this point category, include a triangular and a willow-leaf form.

All of these projectile points range between one-half and one and one-half inches in length. Eight specimens are side notched, and 2 others exhibit a combination of corner and side notches. One of the latter 2 has 2 sets of notches, with the base being broken at the proximal set. The proximal set is composed of corner notches and the distal set of side notches. Since the break appears to be fresher than the distal set of notches, both sets may have been present at the same time.

Other Flint Artifacts

The main descriptions of the flint artifacts were done in 1956. Since this time I have come into contact with a great deal of additional information on flint-working techniques as well as on flint artifact types. Unfortunately, time and expense did not permit a restudy of the flint from Steuben, but some general observations can be presented here. These are due mainly to the assistance provided by Lewis R. Binford and Mrs. Anta White, research personnel in the Museum of Anthropology, who have published their researches in *Anthropological Papers, No. 19,* "Miscellaneous Studies in Typology and Classification." The main difficulty here is that there is no data from anywhere else with which to compare the Steuben flint. The terms used here are relatively recently coined and their definitions are found in the Binford and White papers.

Hopewell had almost all of the major flint-working techniques found in the Eastern United States. There is evidence present that the proportions of these major techniques, somewhat analogous to a pottery ware level, changed, relatively, through time. From an over-all comparison with the Snyders site in Calhoun County, Illinois, the Steuben flint industry is degenerate, that is, the techniques are slovenly. The Laurentian flint-working technique may be absent and the whole complex appears to be closer to a flint-working technique also found in Point Peninsula. In general, it is closer to the Goodall focus industry of southern Michigan than to that at the Snyders site where there is more pressure flaking present. The disc core and the pyramidal core still persist at Steuben and the block core, as inferred from flakes, is dominant, but the technique is somewhat different from those of the Laurentian and Snyders sites. Perhaps there was a slight difference in the preparation of the block core; but since there are no such cores present in the collection, there is no way of telling what the difference may be. There apparently are no tongue cores at Steuben and at this site the expanding block core blade is very rare. There doesn't appear to be much quarry activity at Steuben, and roughed-out nuclei were probably brought into the site. Many of the flakes are trim flakes which exhibit the bulb of percussion on their inner face, while the negative bulb is on the surface of the biface from which they have been detached.

Triangular Knives (Pl. IX, Fig. 1).—It is difficult to separate scrapers from knives. Many specimens could have served as either or both. In general, however, "knives" show wear flakes bifacially, and "scrapers" exhibit wear flakes unifacially.

Triangular knives were probably either blanks for projectile points, or were used as knives. The latter function is indicated by the consistent shape and size of such specimens, and by evidence of crushing on the blade edges. Of a total of 25 Triangular knives collected at Steuben, only 3 were broken. All are between one and three inches long. They range from one-eighth to three-fourths of an inch thick, the usual thickness being between one-fourth and one-half of an inch. Width is generally one to one and one-half inches. Seven specimens exhibit straight bases and the other 18 exhibit various degrees of convexity. Four knives have straight-sided blades, 13 specimens exhibit curved blade edges, and the other 8 appear much like a conventional knife shape. One of the broken knives exhibits a ground base. Another Triangular knife's base has a unifacially flaked bevel.

Ribbon Flake Knives (Pl. IX, Fig. 2).—A total of 171 Ribbon Flake knives characteristic of Hopewell were found on the surface. Generally they are from one to two inches in length and between one-half and one inch wide. Four of the 171 are two and one-half to three and one-half inches long, and another is only one-half of an inch in length. Usually the longer specimens are more extensively worked.

There are 3 categories of Ribbon Flake knives. The first includes knives which are not retouched but which seem to show signs of use. None of the blades seem to be unused. The minute flake scars exhibited by these specimens can be reproduced by sawing on a piece of wood, and the knives presumably could have been used on bone as well. The second category consists of specimens which seem to have been retouched on one edge, either to produce a backed blade or to obtain a cutting edge. This "retouching" in many cases seems to be of the type which can be reproduced by crushing or battering and, as also in the third category, many times an uneven saw-tooth effect is exhibited. In the third category the blades are worked on both edges, including blades worked on all edges except for the end where the bulb of percussion is present. The breakdown into these three categories is as follows:

Unworked, but seem to be used . . .	76
Worked on one edge	44
Worked on both edges	51
Total	171

End Scrapers (Pl. X, Fig. 1).—Two types of end scrapers are represented at the Steuben site: those manufactured from blades and those made from free flakes. A total of 22 blades were made into end scrapers. From an examination of 3 unfinished specimens, it appears that many of the blades were being purposely broken so that there would be a steep area to flake on the end opposite the bulb of percussion. These scrapers range from one to two and one-half inches long and are between three-fourths to one inch wide. Four blades exhibit very steep cutting edges.

Free flake end scrapers number 23. Some, or many, of these also may have had the end opposite the bulb of percussion prepared for steep flaking by breakage. In addition, most have retouching along the right-hand side, but not along the left, when holding the cutting edge away from the observer. In general, these end scrapers range from one to one and one-half inches in diameter and are from one-eighth to one-half of an inch thick. Four specimens exhibit very steeply worked ends.

Free Flake Scrapers.—Scrapers made from free flakes are classified into the same categories as Ribbon Flake Knives. A total of 31 free flakes are retouched on all edges. The 31 scrapers range up to two and one-half inches in maximum breadth and are usually around one-eighth of an inch in thickness. An additional 19 flakes are worked on one edge only. A total of 45 free flakes exhibit only use flakes. The size range is generally smaller than the flakes worked on all edges. The other 62 flakes in the collections are not worked and do not exhibit any use scars.

Plano-convex Scrapers.—A total of 7 thick flakes were used as scrapers. They are from one-half to one and one-half inches in diameter and one-half to one and one-fourth inches in thickness. One is oval and measures one and one-fourth by one and three-fourths inches. They all may be the tops of pyramidal cores removed to produce a new striking platform, and are similar to what is usually called a "turtle-back scraper."

One exhausted pyramidal core, about three-fourths of an inch in diameter, exhibits wear flakes as a result of being used as a scraper. Since the edges are badly crushed, the presence of an orderly arrangement of definite negative bulbs of percussion has been obscured.

Bifacial Scrapers.--Bifacial scrapers number 15. Generally, the dimensions are one-fourth to one-half of an inch thick, one and one-quarter to two inches long, and one to one and one-fourth inches wide. The 3 in the Museum collection are made on flakes, with subsequent ribbon-like flakes having been removed in a fashion somewhat vaguely reminiscent of a tongue core technique. The edges show the results of removing these large flakes as well as crushing scars which are not a result of removing flakes.

Concave-sided Scrapers.--A total of 6 blades exhibit a concavity on one or more edges. Five have a retouched concavity on the side, 3 being retouched on the lower surface and two on the upper surface of the blades. One of these specimens also has a concavity at the edge opposite the bulb of percussion as does the sixth blade. The concavities range from one-eighth to one-half of an inch across and from one-sixteenth to one-fourth of an inch deep. One blade's concavity is on the side and, rather than being circular in its essential outline, is a sort of diagonal notch.

An additional 12 concave-sided scrapers are made from various types of free flakes. The size range and the shape of the concavities are similar to those exhibited on the blades. One flake has concavities on two sides, opposite each other. Another has a diagonal notch on one edge. Several additional Free Flake scrapers have smaller and shallower concavities, with small flake scars within, and may belong to this same general artifact class.

Gravers.—A total of 4 flint gravers are from the village, 3 of which are made from free flakes. The other is a ribbon flake, measures one and one-half by one inch in extent, and has a small graver point, isolated by small steep retouching, in the center of the end opposite the bulb of percussion. The free flake gravers are around an inch in maximum breadth. A small graver point was isolated on one, and part of a broken flake was pointed slightly by retouching on another. The third free flake graver may have had a point prepared by a technique analogous to the burin technique, with a flake being struck off either side and the resultant point edges being either retouched or scarred through use as a scraper. There are very small scars on all of the graver points where tiny flakes were removed as the tool was used. Several additional flakes exhibit possible graver points, seemingly showing polish or small use flakes at that region. But if they were gravers, they were not prepared in any definite way and were probably used infrequently.

Effigies.—Two flint artifacts were found which apparently had no utilitarian role. Both have a single-flaked surface and appear, with some imagination, much like effigies. One, in a shape reminiscent of a turtle, is two inches long, one and one-fourth inches wide, and one-half of an inch thick. Several notches seem to define a head, four legs, and a tail. This specimen exhibits secondary chipping, showing that some care was taken with its fabrication.

The other flint artifact is one and one-fourth inches long, one-half of an inch wide, and one-fourth of an inch thick. A possible animal head is set off by notches and has been polished to a smooth finish. A tail might be represented by the point which exists beneath the notches. These may actually be effigies, for such artifacts are present at most Hopewell sites.

Unfinished Projectile Point.--In the UMMA collection there is half of a projectile point which was in the process of being manufactured at the time of breakage. Large shallow side notches and a convex base are present. The unfinished point was split almost completely in half from an unlucky blow near the notch on the blade edge. Rather than catching the blade edge just on the other side, the blow must have landed squarely on the edge itself. This artifact exhibits the negative bulb of percussion. Only one of the flake scars exhibited may be the result of pressure flaking.

Hammerstones and/or Cores.--There are 4 thick flakes present whose function is not known. They are two to two and one-half inches in diameter and one inch thick. Another 8 chunks of flint may be cores and/or hammerstones. They are from one to two inches in diameter.

Other Stone Artifacts

Celts (Pl. X, Fig. 2).—Three of the 5 complete celts are made of slate and 2 are of granite. They are fairly flat and quite slender in relation to their length. The bits of 3 of the celts flare slightly. There are also 7 celt polls and 5 bits included in the surface collection. Three of the broken polls suggest a fairly round celt shape in contrast to the rectangular shape of the other specimens.

Gorgets (Pl. XI, Fig. 1).—One complete gorget and 8 fragments show the abundance of this artifact at the Steuben site. In addition, 5 unfinished gorgets were found. These had been crudely shaped and somewhat smoothed but had not yet been drilled. Gorget categories represented are as follows:

Rectangular	3
Oval	2
Reel-shaped	1
Indeterminable	3
Unfinished	5
Total	14

An interesting history can be reconstructed from the only complete gorget. This specimen is two and one-half inches long, but the remnant of a perforation is noticeable at one end. Two perforations near this end attest to two broken pieces having been bound together. Apparently the smaller piece had been lost, the break smoothed over, and another perforation made to salvage the larger fragment as a complete gorget.

Hammerstones (Pl. X, Fig. 2).—A total of 21 pecking stones were collected from the surface of the Steuben site. Their shape varies from round to disc-shaped. One of the 21 exhibits a faint groove and might have been used as a sort of net weight or possibly as a maul. Grooved stones of this sort are found on other Hopewell sites in the Illinois Valley and it is surprising that more were not present at Steuben.

Copper and Galena Artifacts

Only two artifacts of copper were found on the village surface. One was an awl, round in cross section and six and one-half inches long (Pl. XI, Fig. 2). It had been constructed in a shape quite similar to a specimen found in a Hopewell tomb in White County, Illinois (Neumann and Fowler, 1952:206-7, Pl. LXIX, p. 204). One end of the Steuben specimen terminates in a point, and the other is flattened and twisted at an angle. The artifact found in White County is hafted, the pointed end embedded in a deer antler handle and the other end presumably having been used for flint flaking. The other copper specimen is a doubled-over sheet which measures one inch by three-fourths of an inch in extent. A rubbed piece of galena about two and one-half inches in diameter was also found on the surface. This could have been brought in to make either white paint or an artifact comparable to those made of hematite.

Bone Artifacts

For the most part, bone artifacts were utilitarian. One exception is a part of a turtle shell which measures one inch by one-fourth of an inch in extent. This artifact exhibits a complete perforation in its center and another partial perforation on one broken edge. Two sides are ground smooth, suggesting a rattle.

Awls from the surface of the Steuben site number 23 (Pl. XII, Fig. 2). Where it is possible to discern, the distal end of a deer metatarsal is the butt of the awl with one exception which seems to have been made from a deer ulna. The awl categories are the following:

Mammal Leg Bones	
Head of bone intact.	3
Splinter, single-pointed	5
Splinter, double-pointed.	4
Indeterminable	6
Total	18
Bird Bones	
Head of bone intact (split)	2
Indeterminable	3
Total	5
Total Awls	23

Antler Artifacts

A total of four antler artifacts show possible signs of having been hafted, though unfortunately all four are broken at their basal ends. One is a broken-pointed artifact, probably originally a barbed antler tine, whose bore almost reaches the point and which is two and one-half inches long. An unfinished specimen is three inches long and exhibits the beginnings of a drilling process on its flattened base. A broken handle or flaking implement is two inches in length and has a one-inch deep bore. The fourth specimen is seven inches long, has a bore which is one inch in depth, and is either a broken flaking implement or a handle.

Three other antler artifacts, all five inches in length, are unbored and have polished points or tips. All three were broken off at about the base of the deer rack and were probably used as flaking implements. In addition, an antler drifter was found which is four and one-fourth inches long and one and one-half inches in diameter (Pl. XII, Figs. 1 and 2). No evidence of battering is present on this specimen or on the majority of similar artifacts in Illinois sites. Rather than being flaking implements which is the most common functional interpretation concerning such artifacts, they must have had another function, as yet unknown.

Shell Artifacts

Artifacts of shell consisted entirely of hoes and spoons. Spoons found in the village site are fragmentary and rare, but broken and complete hoes are fairly numerous. Hoes range in size from three to six and one-half inches long and from two and one-half to four inches wide. None of the spoons are complete enough to show either the presence or absence of notches on the handles. The collections contain three fragmentary spoons, 10 complete hoes, and 5 broken hoes.

OTHER SURFACE COLLECTIONS FROM THE VILLAGE

The first intensive collector at the Steuben site is reported to have visited the site while working as a foreman of a highway crew. No one knows what, or how much, he found, and the collection seems to have been dispersed long ago. Several individuals have visited the site but what many of these people found will probably never be known. "Collections made in earlier years must have contained many fine pieces because the casual collector generally picks up only perfect items and chert was so plentiful on the site. Large specimens of the fine Hopewellian blades are among items reported" (Schoenbeck, 1948:20). Several fine specimens are rumored to have been found at the Steuben site at around the turn of this century. But the majority of these reports seem to be mostly myth, especially when compared to what is known to have been found there during the past thirty years.

Messrs. Virginius H. Chase and Leroy Elliot began collecting from the Steuben Village site in 1930 and 1933, respectively. George and Ethel Schoenbeck began visiting the site in 1939, and gave their collection to the Illinois State Museum just before the death of Ethel Schoenbeck in 1950. I examined the collections of Chase and Elliot, both of Peoria, in December of 1957. Most of the pottery collected by Mr. Chase was given to the University of Illinois in 1955. Dr. James B. Griffin typed 2,000 sherds belonging to the George Schoenbeck collection in 1951, and Ethel Schoenbeck published some details of the collection in three papers in the *Transactions of the Illinois Academy of Science* (Schoenbeck, 1947, 1948, and 1949). In addition, Cameron has published on the stone artifacts from the Schoenbeck collection in the Illinois State

Museum (Cameron, 1953). This is all of the information on the Schoenbeck collection that I have, as the collection was inaccessible when I visited the Illinois State Museum in 1956 for the purpose of examining it.

Pottery

Table XIV indicates that none of these three collections represent random samples because Weaver and undecorated sherds, generally, seem to have been avoided. Some of the sherds indicate minor post-Hopewell camp site occupations at the Steuben site. A Maples Mills occupation is inferred from the presence of Blumenshein Cord Impressed and eleven Mossville Cordmarked sherds. Middle Mississippi is represented by two Cahokia Cordmarked sherds.

TABLE XIV

POTTERY TYPES IN THE ELLIOT, CHASE, AND SCHOENBECK COLLECTIONS FROM THE STEUBEN VILLAGE SITE

Type	Chase Collection	Elliot Collection	Schoenbeck Collection	Total
Havana Cordmarked	34	69	437	540
Havana Plain	29	32	136	197
Naples Dentate Stamped	6	13	18	37
Hummel Dentate Stamped	7	26	66	99
Hummel Plain Stamped	-	-	5	5
Havana Zoned Dentate Stamped	-	3	26	29
Havana Zoned Incised	-	-	2	2
Havana Plain Rocked Stamped	1	-	-	1
Havana Dentate Rocked Stamped	1	-	-	1
Steuben Punctated	20	45	555	620
Victory Brushed	1	-	8	9
Neteler Dentate Crescent Stamped	-	-	1	1
Havana Miscellaneous Incised	-	-	73	73
Indeterminable	1	1	-	2
Total Havana	100	189	1327	1616
Weaver Cordmarked	5	12	283	300
Weaver Plain	2	1	223	226
Weaver Notched Rim	1	-	-	1
Weaver Incised	1	-	-	1
Weaver Miscellaneous Incised	1	-	-	1
Weaver Miscellaneous Punctated	1	-	-	1
Weaver Punctated Lip	1	-	-	1
Total Weaver	12	13	506	531

TABLE XIV (Continued)

Type	Chase Collection	Elliot Collection	Schoenbeck Collection	Total
Hopewell Plain	-	-	11	11
Hopewell Rim	-	2	12	14
Hopewell Plain Rocked Stamped	-	1	3	4
Hopewell Zoned Plain Rocked Stamped	-	-	7	7
Hopewell Zoned Incised	-	-	3	3
Hopewell Zoned Dentate Stamped	-	-	4	4
Hopewell Incised	-	-	6	6
Hopewell Brushed	-	-	5	5
Hopewell Zoned Brushed	-	-	1	1
Baehr Plain	-	-	1	1
Baehr Incised	-	-	14	14
Baehr Zoned Punctated	-	-	4	4
Baehr Zoned Brushed	-	-	5	5
Brangenberg Plain	-	-	2	2
Montezuma Punctated	-	2	1	3
Hopewell Red Filmed	-	-	8	8
Baehr Dentate Rocked Stamped	-	-	6	6
Baehr Plain Rocked Stamped	-	-	20	20
Baehr Brushed	-	1	38	39
Total Hopewell	-	6	154	160
Blumenshein Cord Impressed	-	-	1	1
Mossville Cordmarked	-	-	11	11
Cahokia Cordmarked	-	1	1	2
Total Other	-	1	13	14
Total	112	209	2000	2321

Several sherds with Weaver paste and thickness in the Chase collection have attributes reflecting possible Hopewell ware ancestry. One sherd has a cordmarked body, a crosshatched upper rim bounded at the base of the design by an incised line, and a zoned plain decoration on the lower rim and the shoulder. Only parts of two zoned plain areas in the shape of circles are on the sherd, hence the design could be a zoned cordmarked motif. A second sherd has a series of deep circular punctates on a slightly beveled lip. The punctates are spaced about one-fourth of an inch apart. The rim is slightly channeled and is cordmarked over the exterior surface. Beneath the channel, there is a broad, shallow, incised line. Two "plain" body sherds also in the Chase collection have respectively a crudely incised X and a randomly punctated treatment on the exterior surfaces.

One of the Naples Dentate Stamped sherds in the Elliot collection also has plain stamping on the exterior surface. The Hopewell Plain Rocked Stamped sherd in the Elliot collection also has some dentate rocked stamped units within the major design. All three of the Montezuma Punctated sherds in Table XIV are grit tempered.

The motifs of 90 of the Steuben Punctated sherds and all of the Naples Dentate Stamped specimens in the Schoenbeck collection are superimposed over a cordmarked surface. Five of the 6 Hopewell Incised sherds are grit tempered, and the large incised rim area of each is similar to Mazique Incised in Louisiana (personal communication, Dr. James B. Griffin). In the Schoenbeck collection, 1 Hopewell Zoned Plain Rocked Stamped, 6 Hopewell Plain Rocked Stamped, 3 Hopewell Zoned Incised, and 4 Hopewell Zoned Dentate Stamped sherds are grit tempered. Two of the 12 sherds included in the Hopewell Rim category have a sandy paste. A Hopewell Plain Rocked Stamped rim sherd in the Schoenbeck collection is similar to Chevalier Stamped in Louisiana (personal communication, Dr. James B. Griffin). One of the 2 Brangenberg Plain sherds is incised on the lip.

Projectile Points

The examination of three large separate collections of projectile points at three different times in three different places resulted in some interesting considerations of my types (Table XV). Messrs. Elliot's and Chase's collections were typed quickly on two successive days, almost two years after I had typed the Morse and UMMA Collection. The general over-all consistency and five specific consistencies indicate two things: (1) the samples are equally random; and (2) the same physical attributes are being consistently used. It does not demonstrate, of course, that the types are or are not valid. The two varieties of the Large Side Notched category are not satisfactory; that is, the results of the samples are not entirely consistent. Since the same sort of sample differentiation is present for the Small Triangular category, and the difference is opposite that in the Large Side-Notched category, it is apparent that these three series are not being segregated on the basis of consistently used attributes. In addition, a very major sample difference occurs within the Steuben Expanded Stemmed, variety long and slender, category. Sample differences are also found within the three varieties of Marshall Barbed and Contracting and Straight Stemmed, variety straight

TABLE XV

PROJECTILE POINTS FROM THE SURFACE OF THE STEUBEN VILLAGE SITE

Type	Chase Collection		Elliot Collection		Morse and UMMA Collection		Combined Collection	
	Number	Per Cent	Number	Per Cent	Number	Per Cent	Number	Per Cent
Snyders Corner Notched	6	4.58	11*	5.24	11	5.26	28	5.09
Marshall Barbed, variety fine	9	6.87	18	8.57	23	11.00	50	9.09
Marshall Barbed, variety rugged	3	2.29	1	0.48	7	3.35	11	2.00
Marshall Barbed, variety crude	-	-	3	1.43	9	4.31	12	2.18
Steuben Expanded Stemmed, variety long and slender	37	28.25	71	33.82	25	11.97	133	24.19
Steuben Expanded Stemmed, variety squat and thick	7	5.34	10	4.76	13	6.22	30	5.45
Steuben Expanded Stemmed, variety small and thin	10	7.63	15	7.14	14	6.70	39	7.09
Large Side Notched, variety straight and concave base	12	9.16	25	11.90	32	15.31	69	12.55
Large Side Notched, variety convex base	20	15.27	21	10.00	32	15.31	73	13.28
Contracting and Straight Stemmed, variety pointed base	-	-	2	0.95	4	1.91	6	1.09
Contracting and Straight Stemmed, variety rounded base	6	4.58	8	3.81	9	4.31	23	4.18
Contracting and Straight Stemmed, variety straight base	3	2.29	4	1.90	17	8.13	24	4.36
Small Triangular	18*	13.74	21*	10.00	13	6.22	52	9.45
Total	131	100.00	210	100.00	209	100.00	550	100.00

*An asterisk indicates that drills or scrapers are included in that category.

base, all of which are very closely related in type to the long and slender variety of Steuben Expanded Stemmed. These differences indicate that Steuben Expanded Stemmed, variety long and slender, and, Contracting and Straight Stemmed, variety straight base, should be combined into a single category. In addition, a finer analysis of the varieties in Marshall Barbed, Large Side Notched, and Small Triangular, should be made.

Cameron (1953) typed 376 projectile points contained in the Schoenbeck collection from the Steuben site. Unfortunately, his types neither conform to my types nor do they always conform to Cameron's illustrated representatives. I suspect, further, that the Illinois State Museum did not get all of the Schoenbeck collection because of the many discrepancies between Ethel Schoenbeck's descriptions and those of Cameron (Schoenbeck, 1948:20).

Other Flint Artifacts

Cameron (1953) doesn't mention the bird effigy made of pink flint which was found by the Schoenbecks (Schoenbeck, 1948:20). However, Mr. Elliot found another made of a mottled grey and white flint which is almost identical to the Schoenbeck specimen (personal communication, Mr. Leroy Elliot [Pl. XIII, Fig. 1]). The Elliot effigy is one and three-fourths inches long, seven-eighths of an inch wide, and three-eighths of an inch thick. Ethel Schoenbeck reported that theirs was two inches in length.

In the Elliot collection are a Snyders Corner-Notched scraper and two small triangular-shaped drills (Table XVI). Three triangular-shaped drills are in the Chase collection. Four of the unidentifiable projectile points in the Chase collection are unfinished.

Other Stone Artifacts

The Chase collection includes a fragment of a rectangular gorget made of hematite, a disc-shaped hammerstone, a slightly pecked and grooved hammerstone or net weight, two grooved quartzite abraders, and a one and one-half-inch-long, triangular-shaped sheet of mica. Two stone celts are also in the Chase collection. One celt is rectangular in shape, five inches long and two inches wide, and polished from the bit upward for two inches of its length. The other celt is roughly rectangular in shape and the bit is twice as wide as the one and one-half-inch-

TABLE XVI

FLINT ARTIFACTS FROM THE SURFACE OF THE STEUBEN VILLAGE IN THE CHASE AND ELLIOT COLLECTIONS

Flint Category	Chase Collection	Elliot Collection	Total
Unidentifiable Broken Projectile Points and Drills	14	51	65
Triangular Knives	13	33	46
Ribbon Flake Knife, variety used	7	49	56
Ribbon Flake Knife, variety worked on one edge	4	13	17
Ribbon Flake Knife, variety worked on both edges	8	21	29
Ribbon Flake End Scraper	2	5	7
Ribbon Flake Scraper with Concave Edge	-	5	5
Free Flake Scraper, variety slightly worked	3	26	29
Free Flake Scraper, variety worked on all edges	25	44	69
Free Flake End Scraper	3	8	11
Plano-convex Scraper	3	5	8
Bifaced Scraper	-	4	4
Total	82	264	346

wide poll. This celt is seven inches long and has a one-half-inch wide polished band completely around the specimen, presumably where it was hafted, from three to three and one-half inches below the poll.

Mr. Elliot has found five celts, though one of these may be a pick. Two are broken and two are unfinished. The only complete celt is six inches long and rectangular in shape with a semi-pointed poll and a straight cutting edge. Two grooved sandstone abraders and a rubbed piece of hematite are in the Elliot collection. There also are three broken slate gorgets in this collection. One gorget is made of red slate and the other two of grey slate. Interestingly, a large, crude, granite flake has had large flakes taken off completely across one face. On the opposite face, which includes the original cortex surface, small flakes have been removed along the edges. The specimen is percussion-flaked and one end still retains the manufactured striking platform. A flat pear-shaped flaked hematite artifact, two and one-fourth by one and one-fourth by seven-sixteenths of an inch thick, is very similar to members of the triangular knife category (Pl. XIV). A grooved teardrop-shaped limestone plummet, one and three-fourths inches long and three-fourths of an inch in diameter, and a granite discoidal with shallow Woodland-like cups with dull edges, two and one-half inches in diameter and one and one-fourth inches thick, are also in the Elliot collection (Pl. XIII, Figs. 2 and 3).

Similar smaller discoidals, made of sandstone, are found on the Nutwood site which is located in the southern part of the Illinois Valley. The Nutwood Village site is multicomponent; the major component present is Early Jersey Bluff, just post-Hopewell, and the minor component represented is Late Archaic (possibly Titterington focus). Both handled pipe and platform pipe forms are found in the village; however, the platform pipe form is similar to a specimen found in one of the Bluff Culture mounds on a bluff overlooking the site. The pipe platform is straight in shape, and oval to round in cross section. Hopewell pipes of this class are usually curved-based with a convex-concave cross-sectioned platform. There are good indications that Copena is Late Hopewell. Interestingly, a limestone-tempered pottery discoidal was found in a Copena burial (Webb and DeJarnette, 1952: 278). Other "discoidals" found in Copena are made of galena.

Ethel Schoenbeck reports they had found 15 fragments of oblong pendants, "a few celts and axe portions," many pitted hammerstones, ball-shaped chert pecking stones, a few shaped disks, and several grooved "mauls" (Schoenbeck, 1948:20-21). Cameron, in discussing the Schoenbeck collection, reported the presence of 17 gorget fragments and a grooved axe, though he refers to Figure 38A, which is a maul (Cameron, 1953). The Schoenbecks also found a white flint marble-like object, eleven-sixteenths of an inch in diameter (Schoenbeck, 1942:46), and a human head effigy made of argillaceous sandstone: "It (the human head effigy) is a portion of some larger object, possibly a figurine, and measures in height 22 millimeters. Details offered by the effigy include the type of features and facial contour; the shape of the head and the shaved scalp; the elaborately ornamented or highly conventionalized ear; and the indication of some accouterment breaking the line between neck and left shoulder." (Schoenbeck, 1947:41, note Fig. 2).

Two grooved axes have been described to me by residents neighboring the Steuben site. One axe found years ago is reported as coming from the village. The other was found about 500 yards west of Mound 1, in 1954, while planting fir saplings. I was not able to inspect either of the two axes.

The presence of a plummet and two grooved axes in addition to the absence of Early Woodland pottery indicate the probability of a minor preceramic component at the Steuben site. Plummets, however, may have lasted from Late Archaic through Hopewell into Jersey Bluff in south-central Illinois. But grooved axes in the Eastern United States seem to be confined to around the Mississippi River and west during Middle and Late Hopewell times (Mohrman and Mohrman, 1950:58, and Griffin, 1955). Very few grooved axes have been reported east of this area in Hopewell and their inclusion in a Hopewell assemblage at a few sites may well be due to the aborigines finding an artifact dating from earlier times, or to accidental association. For example, nobody would consider the curved-based platform pipe found associated with a burial at the Fiedler site, Fulton County, Illinois, as a Middle Mississippi trait (Morse, Schoenbeck, and Morse, 1953:39).

Other Artifacts

Mr. Chase has a fragment of a bone awl in his collection. Mr. Elliot's collection contains an unperforated shell hoe, with the hinge ground down; a barbed antler artifact, three inches long; the points of two bone awls; two broken and used antler tines; and a broken, split mammal leg bone which was highly polished from use, probably as a scraper. All the bone artifacts appear to have been manufactured from deer bone. The Schoenbeck collection included at least four bone awls, one cut antler artifact, and two shell hoes (Schoenbeck, 1948:20-21).

MOUND EXCAVATIONS

Directly to the west of the village site are two bluffs, separated by an unnamed creek, upon which are nine mounds. Seven of the mounds had been previously excavated. We could find no local traditions concerning the identity of the excavators, thus inferring that the digging had been done some time ago. Fortunately, a clue was found as to a possible identity (Spooner, 1940:8), and Dr. Morse followed this up with appropriate research in 1958. According to three articles in the *Peoria Daily Transcript* (reproduced as Appendixes F, G, and H) in September and October of 1877, members of the Peoria Scientific Association and some friends excavated five mounds located on a bluff a short distance south of Sparland, which is the location of the Steuben site. At that time, the Association was planning next to excavate in what must be the present Dickison Mound Group. The first mound explored by this association at Steuben contained a group of four burials with an associated pottery vessel. Further excavations in the same mound resulted in the finding of additional child and adult remains and two perforated bear teeth. The other four mounds explored by the Association contained only charred bone.

The Peoria Scientific Association held their meetings in the basement of the Peoria County Court House, but disbanded a little before the turn of the century because the space was needed for county functions (personal communication, Mr. Virginius Chase). In the hopes of finding the artifacts collected at Steuben by the Association, Dr. Morse began diligent searches in the Peoria Library, Bradley University, and other likely places. The only artifact located in these searches was a small Steuben Punctated vessel in the collection of the Peoria Historical Society. All that is known is that the vessel has been there for a number of years and was obtained from the Peoria Scientific Association. This probably is the vessel referred to in the *Peoria Daily Transcript*.

The Peoria Scientific Association vessel is 4.5 inches high and varies between 5.25 and 5.5 inches in diameter. It has two horizontal rows of small Steuben Punctates immediately below the lip, and is grit tempered with many mica fragments included in the Weaver-like paste. Other attributes are a sharp inward beveled lip, a constricting mouth, and a round base. It is similar to the so-called "coconut" shape.

Five of the six mounds on the southern bluff at the Steuben site had been previously excavated and the excavations filled afterwards. Two of the three mounds on the northern bluff were dug and the holes left open. In one of the holes and in the dirt removed from it there was a considerable amount of mussel shell. No mention of mussel shell was made in the previously mentioned newspaper accounts. Hence, the Peoria Scientific Association probably dug five of the six mounds on the southern bluff at Steuben late in 1877. The artifacts obtained are comparable to those secured by my father and me in Mound 1. The mention of charred bone in four of the mounds is a little puzzling, since none was found when we tested or completely excavated the previously dug mounds. However, since we found almost no skeletal material at all in those mounds, much of the bone may have been kept by the Association. The excavations on the northern bluff appear much more recently done than those on the southern bluff, but as yet we have no clue concerning the identity of the excavators.

Mounds 2 through 9

On the bluff to the north of the creek are three oval mounds, numbers 7, 8, and 9. All three are approximately 60 to 70 feet long and 20 to 30 feet wide. They range from 3 to 5 feet in height. Two, Mounds 8 and 9, are all but completely destroyed by previous excavation. Mound 7, which is not definitely a mound, was only slightly pitted by previous explorers. We did not test excavate any of these three mounds.

Mound 5 is about 45 feet long, 30 feet wide, and 4 feet high. Mound 6 is a little smaller than Mound 5 but is roughly the same shape. Although there was little external evidence of disturbance in both mounds, they were found to have been almost completely dug by previous excavators. No skeletal remains were found by us in the process of completely bulldozing both mounds down in the spring of 1956.

Mound 4 is approximately 30 feet in diameter and 3 to 4 feet high. External signs of disturbance were not major for Mound 4 either; but only a few very fragmentary and decayed bones were found in a previously disturbed central subfloor burial pit.

Mound 3 is 4 feet high and about 35 to 40 feet in diameter. We excavated a trench through the entire mound despite the presence of a large hole in the summit. The general make-up of the mound is a dark loam primary mound over a subfloor burial pit with a light loam secondary capping. Two recently disturbed and very poorly preserved child skeletons were found in what appeared to be a shallow round burial pit about 5 feet in diameter. The cross section of the trench indicated that the previous excavation had not been extensive enough to have destroyed the essential outline of the burial pit. Among the bones was a broken unworked beaver jaw.

About the same shape and size as Mound 3, Mound 2 also consisted of a dark loam primary mound and a light loam secondary mantle. In Mound 2 the central feature, apparently a subfloor burial pit, was found to have been completely destroyed by previous explorers. Only a few adult skull fragments and several large stones were present in the center of the mound. The stones probably either were placed there by the excavators while refilling the hole or were used by the mound builders for keeping a mat in place, perhaps upon a log tomb roof.

Mound 1

Mound 1 is the largest in the group of nine mounds (Pl. XV, Figs. 1 and 2). It is 103 feet long and 38 feet wide. The mound reaches a maximum height of 5 feet, 8 inches near its northern end. Excavations began in the fall of 1952, and by the spring of 1955 a trench ranging between 5 and 9 feet in width traversed 88 feet of its length. In addition, a cross trench was dug completely through the northern end, and in the center of the mound a trench was excavated through the western side. In the spring of 1956, the unexcavated parts of the mound were removed with the help of a small bulldozer.

The eastern slope of Mound 1 merges with the slope of the bluff. Around the rest of the mound circumference there seems to be a depressed area which is probably where the mound fill was obtained. At least 58 individuals were buried in Mound 1. In addition, several other individuals are represented only in part; that is, there were disarticulated bones found scattered throughout the central portion of the oval mound which showed no apparent relationship to each other, nor to any of the frequently encountered incomplete burials. These loose bones probably are the result of disturbance by woodchucks and by the mound builders. Some of the bones may represent the lone remnants of secondary or scaffold burials. The fill of Mound 1 was so hard that only two short-lived attempts had been made by previous explorers to excavate the mound. Neither of the two shallow holes seems to have encountered, and thus disturbed, any burials.

A general reconstruction of Mound 1 can be construed from Figures 2 and 3. Briefly, a north to south oriented series of three primary conical mounds were constructed, enlarged, and finally joined into one oval mound. The southernmost primary mound covered Burial Pit D, the central primary mound was constructed over Burials Pits A and B and a small empty pit, and the northernmost primary mound overlay Burial Pit C. A small conical mound was constructed over the gulf between the central primary mound and the multiple-capped southern primary mound, and covered a bundle burial group. A dirt cap was added on top of this mound and the southern gulf filled in. A secondary mound was constructed over the central primary mound, and later, apparently, the top of the secondary mound was utilized to fill in the northern gulf and the collapsed center of the northern primary mound (Fig. 5). The final mantle of soil resulted in a large symmetrical oval mound. In every instance of soil addition, burials were made in the mound.

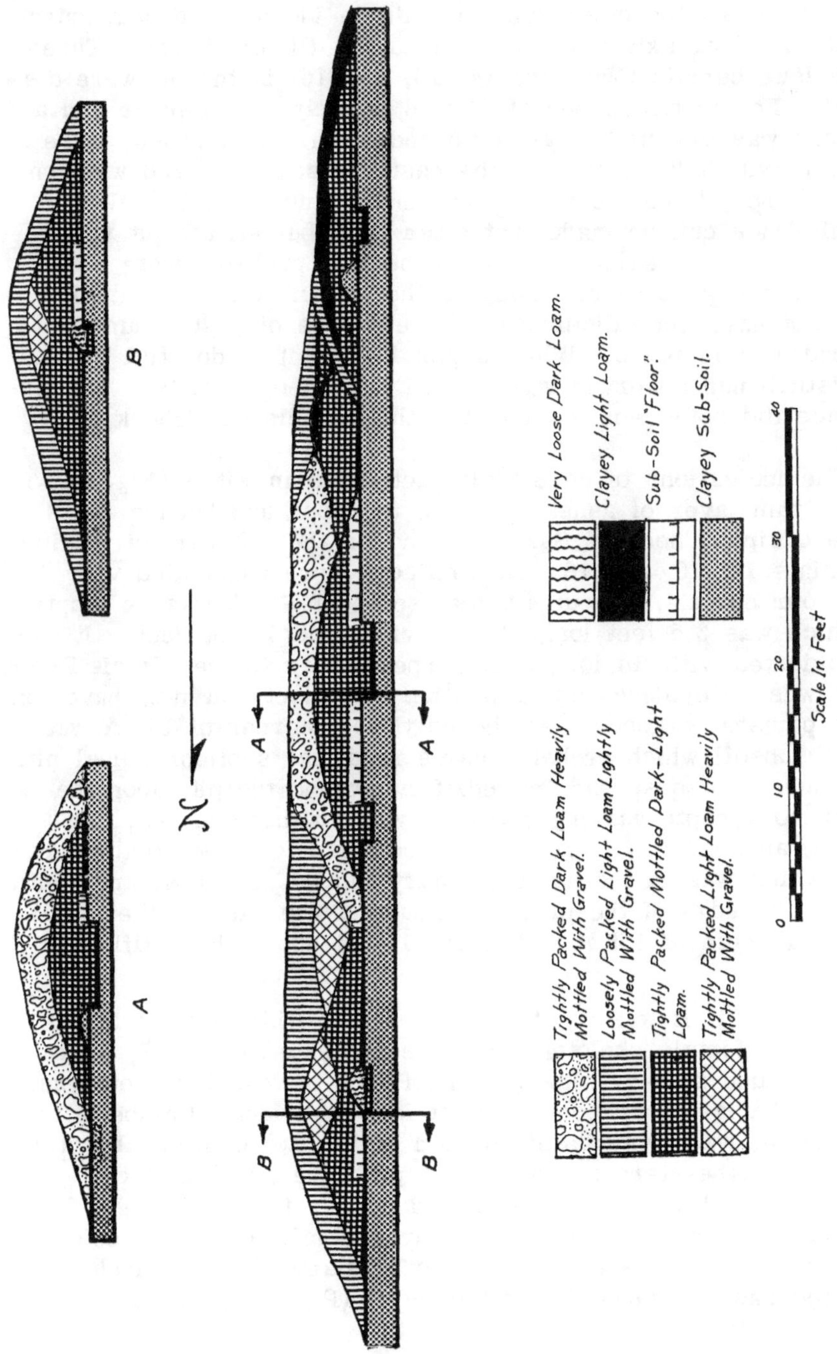

Fig. 5. Profiles of Mound 1 at the Steuben Site.

Pit A.—Pit A was 6.5 feet long, 6 feet wide, and 10 inches deep. Like all the other subfloor pits in Mound 1, it was oriented with its long axis perpendicular to the Illinois River. Three of the four burials (Numbers 14, 15, and 16) in the pit were disturbed. For instance, one skull was slightly out of place and a humerus was oriented straight up and down. In addition, there was a rodent hole in each of the eastern, southern, and western sides of the pit, one of which contained a human tibia. Hence, the inference can be made that after each burial, the pit was refilled. Thus, the earlier burial or burials probably were disturbed in the process of redigging the pit and the last burial would not have been disturbed. No evidence of post-Columbian exploration was found. While a possibility, it is doubtful that all the disturbance observed was caused by rodent activity. The disturbance did not seem consistent with probable woodchuck burrows.

The indications of ceremonial activities in Pit A (Fig. 6) were a thin layer of ashes upon the pit floor and burned areas on the occipital bone of Burial 13 and on the left parietal region of Burials 14, 15, and 16. No artifacts were associated with these four burials. About 4.5 feet south of Pit A was an empty pit which was 3.5 feet long, 2 feet wide, and 1 foot deep. It was also oriented with its long axis perpendicular to the Illinois River. There was no evidence as to whether the empty pit may have contained perishable goods. At the northwest corner of Pit A was a pile of subsoil which probably came from the subfloor burial pit. More subsoil was spread immediately around the pit, upon the topsoil, to a depth varying between two and three inches, thus creating an artificial floor. This floor was followed northward to Pit B which was in the same primary mound as Pit A, and southward to the edge of the primary mound. The base of the small empty pit south of Pit A was about 1 foot above the artificial floor.

Pit B.—Pit B was 6.5 feet long, 3 feet wide, and 10 inches deep. Two female skeletons, Burials Number 21 and 22, were lying extended side-by-side within an inch of touching shoulders. A bundle burial group consisting of four individual (Numbers 17 through 20), was immediately on top of the two extended burials. Near the northeastern corner of the pit were found a notched shell spoon and a scrap of unworked copper (Pl. XVI, Figs. 1 and 2). Between the two pelves were three small pottery vessels.

The smallest vessel is 4 inches in diameter and 4 inches high, and has a Steuben Punctated motif (Pl. XVII, Fig. 1). Two

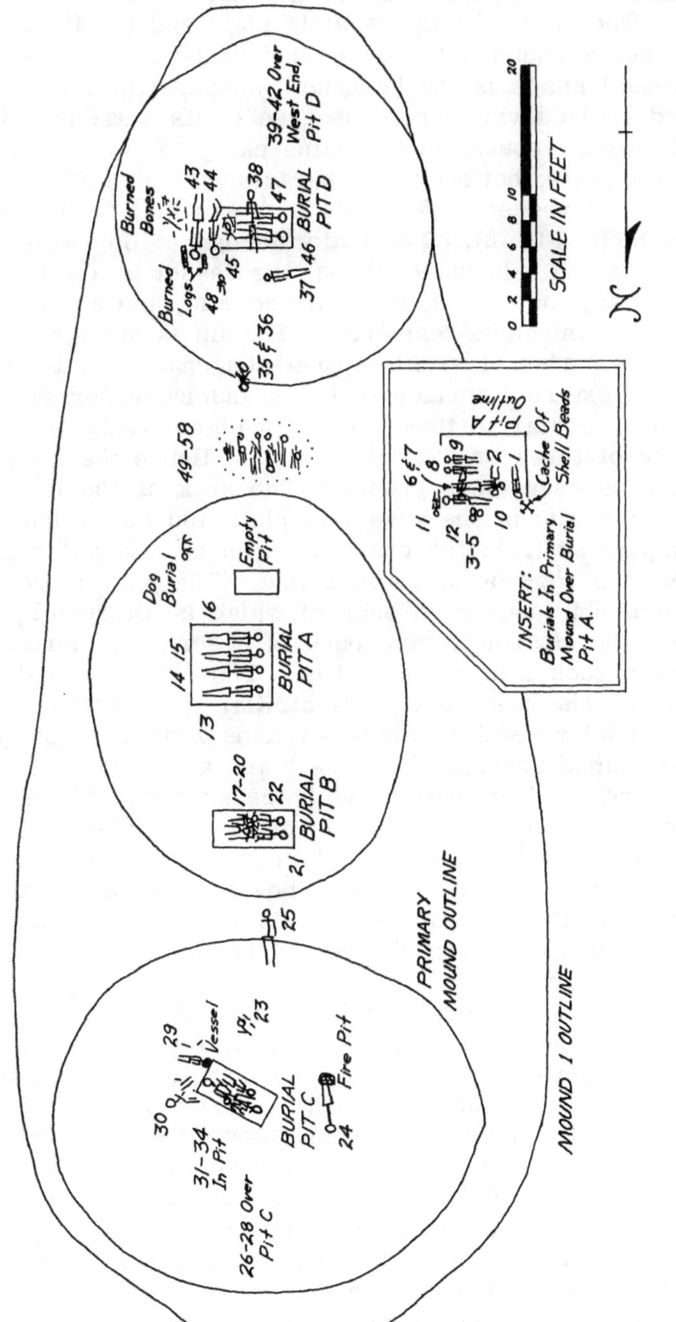

Fig. 6. Burials in Mound 1 at the Steuben Site.

horizontal rows of punctates are present on the rim just beneath the lip. The body of the vessel is plain and the lip is intermediate between a rounded and a beveled shape in cross section. The basic vessel shape is the "coconut" shape, with a slightly rounded base and an incurving rim. Because of its smallness in comparison with other vessels in the same category, the walls are thin; the vessel paste, however, is characteristic of Havana ware.

A second vessel is 5 inches high and 2.75 inches in diameter (Pl. XVII, Fig. 2). The major design is Hopewell Zoned Plain Rocked Stamped. In basic shape, the vessel is a jar with a rounded base, four lobes, a channeled rim, and an outcurving rim area. It is limestone-tempered. The lip is straight in cross section. A series of evenly-spaced diagonal lines is continuous around the exterior surface of the channeled upper rim. Diagonal lines perpendicular to these occur in eight evenly-spaced groups consisting of three or four lines each. Hence the crosshatching is broken between these groups. The neck or the lower two-thirds of the rim of the vessel is plain and highly burnished, being separated from the channeled rim by triangular punctates and from the body by an incised line. The body is composed of four prominent lobes upon each of which is alternately one of two designs. One design is composed of a series of horizontally oriented plain rocked-stamped motifs. The lobe is zoned by an incised line. The other design is similar to a "bull's-eye." Three evenly-spaced incised contour-like lines zone alternately a plain rocked-stamped area, a plain area, and a second plain rocked-stamped area in that order. With the exception of the vessel base, the remainder of the jar is plain and highly burnished. On the base is a circular area of plain rocked stamping enclosed by an incised line. All the incised lines on this vessel are wide and deep, and the rocked stamping is very closely spaced. The whole exterior surface of the vessel is highly burnished and brown to black in color.

The third vessel found in Pit B is a limestone-tempered bowl with an incurving rounded lip (Pl. XVII, Fig. 3). It is 5.75 inches in diameter and 3 inches high. The main design is also Hopewell Zoned Plain Rocked Stamped. The exterior surface is very highly burnished and red to orange in color. On the rounded base is a circular area which is plain rocked stamped and enclosed by a fine and deep incised line. Just beneath the lip is a horizontal row of punctates which gives the appearance of a single broken line. Just above the maximum body diameter is a horizontal incised line to which are attached eight triangles with their apexes oriented toward the vessel base. The triangles are composed of plain rocked stamping outlined by fine and deep incised lines.

Pit C.—Pit C was 3.5 feet wide, 6.5 feet long, and 10 inches deep, and contained four skeletons (Numbers 31, 32, 33, and 34; Pl. XVIII, and Pl. XIX, Fig. 1). No artifacts were associated with the burials. This may be a family burial since a male, a female, and two children are represented. The condition of the skeletons did not indicate a pit left open for sporadic inhumations and it does not seem entirely feasible that these four would die at the same time by chance alone. If the pit had been left open for sporadic inhumations over a period of time, the skeletons would exhibit differing degrees of deterioration. This is not the case in Pit C.

The fill of Pit C also included the following: a broken mandible indicating an elderly female; three skull fragments—two are infantile and the other suggests a female of about forty or more years of age; nine fragments of adult cervical vertebrae; two fragments of child lumbar vertebrae; an adult clavicle suggesting a male; twenty-four broken ribs which are mostly adult; one adult tarsal; one adult manubrium; epiphyseal plates from a proximal tibia and humerus; a child's femur, radius, and humerus; one adult pubis indicating a female of about fifty years of age; one child's pubis; one child's phalange; diverse and sundry woodchuck bones, fragmentary shell, and unworked stone; one Snyders Corner Notched knife (Pl. XVI, Fig. 1).

Around the western, northern, and eastern sides of the pit was an artificial floor made of subsoil which was very similar to the floor found associated with Pits A and B. Upon the southeastern surface of this floor were the remnants of two individuals (Burials Numbers 29 and 30), and the cranium of a third (an adult). Burial 29 had a Baehr Zoned Brushed vessel overturned at the spot where the missing skull should have been (Pl. XX, Figs. 1 and 2). The vessel contained an unnotched shell spoon. Curiously, both femurs were reversed although all the other bones were articulated, hinting at a partly disintegrated state at the time of burial.

The vessel is 4.5 inches high and 4 inches in diameter. The limestone-tempered jar is black in color. The basic jar shape is almost identical to the vessel found near Pit D except that the one associated with Burial 29 has four lobes. In comparison with the jar found in Pit B, the jar with Burial 29 is squattier and has a much shorter neck and rim area. The lip is straight to slightly beveled in cross section. The channeled rim is brushed mostly horizontally. The short neck which is about the same breadth as the rim is plain and bounded by a fine and deep incised line at its juncture with the rim and the body. Each lobe has two parallel, fine, and shallow contour-like incised lines half way around it. The incision is actually continuous, thus zoning an exaggerated quarter moonlike motif. The zoned areas are highly burnished. The rest of the vessel's exterior surface outside the zoned areas is finely brushed, possibly with twigs, in a random manner.

Four perforated black bear canines were associated with Burial 30 (Pl. XXV, Fig. 2). Each canine is perforated twice on the same surface and each perforation extends to just the nerve cavity. Two were lying amongst the bones and two were six to 12 inches above the bones. According to recent excavations by the Gilcrease Foundation in Pike County, Illinois, directed by Gregory Perino, Steuben Burials 29 and 30 are possible rearticulated burials and the canines may be clasps for a robe.

Other human bones found upon the southeastern surface of the artificial floor around Pit C were the following: a pelvis, an ulna, a proximal end of another ulna, a cervical vertebra, and a rib indicate a child of about ten years of age; a distal portion of a humerus, two ribs, a fragment of a parietal, and a broken metacarpal indicate a female of around forty years of age; and a fairly rugged adult left scapula.

There were two indications that Pit C was originally a hollow tomb. A very large depression in the center of the primary mound might have been the result of a cave-in of this tomb. Two semiflexed skeletons (Burials, Numbers 26 and 27) had been placed in this depression, one lying directly upon the other. At the pelvis of Number 27 (the lowermost skeleton) were a raccoon skull and a small area of fired soil including remnants of two small burned logs. At a point a small distance from the skulls of these two burials was an unworked mussel shell which contained seven small flint chips. Also in this depression over Pit C was a bundle burial of the skeleton of a four- to five-year-old child (Number 28), which was placed a little to the west of the other two burials.

Other human bones found in the depression over Pit C were the following: a fragment of an adult female pelvis and some fragments of an adult scapula and adult ribs; a humerus, a fragment of a pelvis, and one thoracic, and one lumbar vertebra belonging to a preadolescent child; a portion of a young child's humerus; and a dozen very fragmentary infant bones.

Directly over the northern part of Pit C was another indication of a hollow tomb (Pl. XIX, Fig. 2). Here was an area of extremely loosely packed dark loam which was about 1 foot deep and 2 to 3 feet in diameter. This could have been the result of the logs comprising the roof of the tomb deteriorating, with the soil above the logs subsequently gradually flaking away until the southern portion weakened enough for the primary mound center to collapse into the relatively hollowed-out area. However, no evidence such as post molds or log impressions, was found to indicate the method of tomb construction. Other small Hopewell tombs in the Illinois Valley have been found associated with definite log impressions near the tomb edges, and occasionally the same sort of situation as described above for Pit C occurs in these other Illinois tombs.

Pit D.—In Pit D, whose dimensions were the same as Pit B, were three skeletons (Pl. XXI, Figs. 1 and 2). A male and a female were lying extended, shoulders almost touching (Burials, Numbers 46 and 47). At the feet of the two extended skeletons were the remains of another adult female (Burial Number 45 [Pl. XXII, Fig. 1]). This latter skeleton was partly articulated, with various articulated parts distributed randomly within the pit's eastern half. There were no signs of violence upon the bones, and it is inferred that the skeleton was buried in a partly distintegrated condition. The only artifact was a single deer bone splinter awl which was found upon washing the bones of Burial 47.

Around Pit D the ground had been cleared of topsoil. Three feet from its eastern edge was a confused pile of disarticulated burned human bones and several charred logs. There were at least three individuals within a three dimensional burned area of between 2 and 3 feet. Between this burned area and the pit were two skeletons which were lying extended perpendicular to the long axis of the pit (Pl. XXII, Fig. 2). The first skeleton was a partly partly burned adult (Burial Number 43). Between Burial 43 and Pit D was a child. The child's skeleton had fallen into Pit D slightly. Also, the red soil overburden, from a burned area above Pit D, had dipped slightly down into the pit. This condition was apparently due to soil settlement and indicates that Pit D was filled until flush with the subsoil surface before making Burial 43. Three feet north of Pit D were found the fragmentary remains of a foetus lying directly upon the subsoil. There did not seem to be much care taken in the burial of the foetus other than its inclusion in the mound.

Immediately over Pit D, 2 feet high at that point, was a mound of burned soil. This did not extend over far enough to be included in the mound profile. At the highest point of this burned mound was Burial 38. What bones were left were exceedingly burned and this partial cremation had taken place where it was found.

Above the burned mound and 2 feet west of the burned burial, but still over Pit D, were the bones of two children (Numbers 39 and 40) bundled into one pile (Pl. XXIII, Fig. 1). An extended child (Burial Number 41) lay about 1 foot to the north. All three were buried in a pit 4 to 6 inches deep and 2 feet square. Between them was a Hopewell Plain Rocked Stamped vessel (Pl. XXIII, Fig. 2). The jar is 6 inches high and 3.75 inches in diameter, lightly burnished, and black in color. The straight lip is exteriorly notched and the whole exterior surface of the vessel is covered by horizontal bands of wide-spaced plain rocked stamps. It has a channeled rim, is very squat in shape, and is limestone-tempered. Two spoons were in the vessel (Pl. XVI, Figs. 1 and 2). One is made from turtle shell and the other is made from a small mussel shell. The latter spoon, interestingly, was made for the use of a left-handed person. At the skull of the extended child was a conch-shell vessel (*Busycon perversum*) and a polished mammal bone rib spatula artifact which was probably worn in the hair (Pl. XVI, Fig. 1 and Pl. XXIII, Fig. 3). Under this burial pit was another small burial pit intruding into the red burned soil. This latter pit was oval and contained a child skeleton (Burial Number 42 [Pl. XXIV, Fig. 1]).

Burial 37 was found about 3 feet north of Pit D at a depth of only 10 inches below the mound surface, being intrusive into the second cap over the primary mound over Pit D (Pl. XXIV, Fig. 2). With Burial 37 were also found a humerus, two broken radii, two ulnas, a sacrum, a portion of a pelvis, and the head of a femur, all perhaps belonging to an adult female. These bones probably resulted from disturbing another skeleton in the process of burying Number 37.

Between Pits A and D was a group of ten individuals (Numbers 49-58) in a bundle burial group (Pl. XXV, Fig. 1). Lying on top of a small mound about 10 inches high, they were arranged in a sort of oval outline with a skull at one or both ends of the individual piles of bone. In the fill between the small mound over these burials and the twice-capped primary mound over Pit D was a double-bundle burial (Burials Number 35 and 36). This latter was an oval-shaped pile of bones with a skull placed at either end. Below the double-bundle burial were found a cranium, a scapula, an unworked rock, and a shell hoe, all in one pile. The remains were fragmentary and the only information obtainable from them was that this individual was an adult.

Other Burials.—Twelve burials were found lying directly upon the primary mound which covered Pits A and B. All were more or less over Pit A. Burials Number 1 through 5 were at the highest point of the mound, being buried at a depth of only 2 feet below the surface of Mound 1. The first two were an infant and a child lying side-by-side about a foot apart. One and one-half feet northeast of these were three adult skulls (Burials 3, 4, and 5).

Three feet directly south of the skulls, at a depth of 3 feet, was a female (Number 6). Her pelvis contained an infant in breech position (Number 7), this undoubtedly being the cause of her death. One and one-half, and 3 feet farther south, respectively, were a child and an infant (Burials 8 and 9).

Burial 10 was 4 feet deep and 1.5 feet north of the mother and infant. A grooved bear canine was at either side of the skull (Pl. XXV, Fig. 2). On the left was a child and also, a little above the head, was another child (Burials Number 11 and 12, respectively). Two and one-half feet farther west was a pile of nineteen small shell beads which were unassociated with any burial (Pl. XXV, Fig. 2). The beads were in, rather than on top of, the primary mound over Pit A.

Almost exactly between Pits B and C lay an extended female skeleton (Burial 25). This skeleton was in a small mound which was built in the gulf between the primary mounds over Pits B and C. Burial 25 was missing a right arm, a maxilla and mandible, and most of the thoracic vertebrae and corresponding ribs. Further north, about 3 feet below the surface of Mound 1, were some fragments of a skull, pelvis, phalanges, vertebrae, and ribs. These suggest a male in his forties. Four feet west of Pit C, at a depth of 3.5 feet, was found a shell hoe (Pl. XXVI, Fig. 1). Another shell hoe was uncovered just south of Pit C and 3 feet below the surface of Mound 1. Neither of the two hoes was associated with a burial. Also in this area were found various fragments of flint, a complete turkey leg, which was flexed and buried upright, and a few Weaver Cordmarked body sherds.

About 4 feet south of Pit C and 2 feet below the Mound 1 surface were found a cranium, a humerus, the proximal ends of a radius and an ulna, and several ribs, metacarpals, and phalanges. Associated with these were some fragments of a Weaver Cordmarked jar with a wavy rim (Pl. XXVI, Fig. 2). Since there seemed to be no indication of a pit, the burial (Number 23) probably took place during the last stage of mound building. Also, it is probable that the remains were disturbed since both the bones and the sherds were scattered over a large area. Some 5 feet south of this, in the primary mound, lay a Steuben Punctated rim sherd and a child's phalange. A few adult fragments of a cranium, scapula, humerus, and several ribs were found about eight and one-half feet north of Burial Number 23.

Burial 24, a male in his fifties, was found about 4 feet west of Pit C directly upon the primary mound (Pl. XXVII, Fig. 1). Missing from the skeleton were both arms, the right scapula and clavicle, and both the maxilla and the mandible. In addition, the neck was twisted abnormally, but since only the second and third thoracic vertebrae were fused together it apparently was not a condition obtained during life. It seems improbable, however, that any disturbance took place after burial since the skeleton was lying extended upon its back with both arms missing. Because nothing could be found on the existing bones, which were not disturbed, that would indicate violence, Number 24 may have been in a partly disintegrated state at the time of burial. Unfortunately the skull was stolen before the skeleton had been completely uncovered and hence could not be submitted to a laboratory analysis for evidence that Burial 24 had been violated during life. A circular pit, 2 feet in diameter and 4 inches deep, was found directly beneath the feet and contained a few small fragments of charcoal and a few small burned rocks. Two and one-half feet beneath the surface of Mound 1, in the gulf between the primary mound over Pits A and B and the secondary mound which covered the large bundle burial group, was a medium-sized dog.

Mound 1 Burial Analyses

The remains of 58 individuals who could be tabulated as to age, sex, stature, and bone pathology were found (Table XVII). The first 12 burials were not collected for laboratory analysis and only a general description of these 12 skeletons can be made from field notes. The limitations of a project of this nature are numerous. Nothing can be told with absolute certainty because of the variability of the individual in growth, nutrition, and perhaps even race. Although the criteria used in this paper have been taken from studies made upon Caucasians, they seem to compare favorably with studies which have been made upon nonwhite groups (Flecker, 1954:98).

TABLE XVII

BURIAL DATA FROM MOUND 1 AT THE STEUBEN SITE

Orientation is from feet to head

Number	Sex	Age	Stature	Depth	Pathology	Orientation	Comments
1	Ch.	1	-	2'		S-N	Not saved for laboratory analysis.
2	Ch.	6	-	2'		S-N	Not saved for laboratory analysis.
3	M	35	-	2'		Bundle	Only the skull and first three vertebrae of 3, 4, and 5 present. 4 and 5 not saved for laboratory analysis.
4	Ad.	-	-	2'		Bundle	
5	Ad.	-	-	2'		Bundle	
6	F	-	-	3'	7 was in breech presentation in pelvis of 6.	E-W	Not saved for laboratory analysis.
7	Ch.	-	-	3'		E-W	Not saved for laboratory analysis.
8	Ch.	12	-	3'		W-E	Not saved for laboratory analysis.
9	Ch.	1-2	-	3'		W-E	Not saved for laboratory analysis.
10	Ad.	-	-	4'		W-E	Not saved for laboratory analysis. Grooved bear canine at each ear.
11	Ch.	3	-	4'		S-N	Not saved for laboratory analysis.
12	Ch.	3	-	4'		S-N	Not saved for laboratory analysis.
13	F	47-52	5'3"	6½'	Bony spur on left femur.	E-W	In Pit A. Undisturbed. Moderate cradle-board deformation.
14	M	50+	5'9"	6½'	Bowed femurs.	E-W	In Pit A. Disturbed. Pronounced cradle-board deformation.
15	F	42-47	5'7"	6½"		E-W	In Pit A. Disturbed. Pronounced cradle-board deformation.
16	F	41-46	5'8"	6½"	Green-stick fracture of right humerus.	E-W	In Pit A. Disturbed.
17	Ch.	2-2½	-	6'		Bundle	17: Moderate cradle-board deformation. 19 and 20: cranium missing. 17-20 were in a group bundle burial directly upon 21 and 22.
18	Ch.	2	-	6'		Bundle	
19	M	50+	5'5"	6'		Bundle	
20	F	30-35	5'6"	6'		Bundle	
21	F	19-20	5'3"	6½'		E-W	21 and 22 in Pit B; associated with one Steuben Punctated and two Hopewell Zoned Plain Rocked Stamped vessels. 21 in Pit B, north side. Pronounced cradle-board deformation. 22 in Pit B, south side. Moderate cradle-board deformation.
22	F	45-50	5'5"	6½"		E-W	
23	F	50+	5'4"	2'		Bundle	Associated with Weaver Cordmarked sherds.
24	M	50+	5'7"	2'	2d and 3d thoracic vertebrae fused.	S-N	Missing both arms, mandible and right shoulder.
25	F	35-40	5'9"	4'		N-S	Disturbed. Pronounced cradle-board deformation.
26	M	14	-	4'		S-N	26 was flexed and lying directly upon 27 (also flexed) in depression over Pit C.
27	F	30-35	5'3"	4'		S-N	27 had moderate cradle-board deformation.
28	Ch.	4-5	-	4'		Bundle	In depression over Pit C.
29	Ch.	2-2½	-	5½'		E-W	At edge of Pit C. Associated with a Baehr Zoned Brushed vessel.

TABLE XVII (Continued)

Number	Sex	Age	Stature	Depth	Pathology	Orientation	Comments
30	Ch.	9-10	-	5½'		Bundle	NE of 29; associated with two perforated bear canines.
31	F	50+	5'5"	6½'		NW-SE	In Pit C.
32	M	35-40	5'4"	6½'		SE-NW	In Pit C.
33	Ch.	8	-	6½'		SE-NW	In Pit C.
34	Ch.	4-5	-	6½'		NW-SE	In Pit C.
35	M	35-40	5'8"	1½-3'	Osteoarthritis of Metatarsal.	Bundle	35 and 36 were together. 35, Pronounced cradle-board deformation.
36	F	16-17	-	1½-3'		Bundle	36, Pronounced cradle-board deformation.
37	M	45-50	5'9"	10"	Healed fracture of 12th thoracic and 1st lumbar vertebrae.	W-E	Remnants of another individual with this burial. Moderate cradle-board deformation.
38	Ad.	40	-	1'		N-S	Burned, fragmentary.
39	Ch.	2½-3½	-	1'		Bundle	39 and 40 together; 39-41 associated with a Hopewell Plain Rocked Stamped vessel, Conch Shell vessel, Turtle Shell and Mussel Shell spoon, and Mammal Bone spatula.
40	Ch.	6-7	-	1'		Bundle	
41	Ch.	1½-2	-	1'		E-W	
42	Ch.	2½-3½	-	2'		S-N	In small pit in red soil. Pronounced cradle-board deformation.
43	M	45-50	5'4"	3'	Arthritis of left knee joint.	S-N	Burned; at edge of Pit D. Moderate cradle-board deformation. Skull and associated log submitted for C-14 analysis.
44	Ch.	5-6	-	3'		S-N	Lying beside 43; fallen part way into Pit D.
45	F	40-45	5'2"	4'	Congenital dislocation of right hip.	Bundle	Partly articulated burial in Pit D.
46	M	21	5'5"	4'		E-W	In Pit D, on north side.
47	F	42-47	5'7"	4'		E-W	In Pit D. Moderate cradle-board deformation.
48	Fetus		-	4'		N-S	Fragmentary.
49	F	42-47	-	4'	Tumor or skull fracture.	Bundle	49-58 were in one group. Moderate cradle-board deformation.
50	M	40-45	5'9"	4'		Bundle	Moderate cradle-board deformation.
51	F	45-50	-	4'		Bundle	Only skull present. Moderate cradle-board deformation.
52	M	45-50	5'8"	4'	Arthritic fusion of 5th lumbar to sacrum.	Bundle	
53	M	45-50	5'11"	4'		Bundle	Very pronounced supraorbital ridges.
54	Ch.	5-6	-	4'		Bundle	Only teeth and pelvis present.
55	M	30-35	5'5"	4'		Bundle	Very pronounced supraorbital ridges. Pronounced cradle-board deformation.
56	M	50+	5'9"	4'	Pronounced osteosclerosis of right tibia.	Bundle	Moderate cradle-board deformation.
57	Ch.	5-6	-	4'	Deformity of right side of skull.	Bundle	
58	Ch.	9-10	-	4'		Bundle	

Sex.—The 58 burials were sorted into 15 males, 16 females, 4 unclassified adults, and 23 children under fourteen years of age (Morse, 1956). It is interesting to note that around 40 per cent of the skeletons found in Mound 1 were children under fourteen years of age. Normally one finds only a few child and infant burials in Hopewell mounds. In my personal experience with other Hopewell mounds in the Illinois Valley, only 10 to 20 per cent of the skeletons were children. Around 30 per cent of the skeletons found in the cemetery at the Wilson site in White County, Illinois, were children (Neumann and Fowler, 1952:218-19).

Age.—The ages of 54 skeletons at time of death were calculated. Of these, 27 were under twenty-one and twenty-seven were over twenty-one years of age. The only appreciable gap between the foetus and the fifty-plus age bracket occurred between twenty-one and about thirty to thirty-five. Neumann (Neumann and Fowler, 1952:218-19, fn.) reports a similar age gap occurring between eleven and twenty-seven in White County, Illinois.

In determining age, I tried to use the data in accordance with its accuracy (Morse, 1957). In children, whose age could be judged by tooth eruption, the estimations are stated in terms of one or two years. The same is done with slightly older individuals who were in varying stages of epiphyseal union. For adults, however, suture closure was not held as being this accurate and, consequently, an estimation of age is in terms of five or ten years.

Children are grouped into ages of .5, 1.5, 2.5, 3.5 ... 21.5, and adults are grouped into ages of 32, 37, 42, 47, and 52, for a determination of the respective means. Six individuals were in their fifties or better. As nothing concrete could be found upon which to base an age over fifty as being accurate, fifty-two was taken as being an appropriate generalization. Two of these six skeletons exhibited extreme molar and premolar loss with subsequent bone absorption; two had only one or two molars missing; and the remaining two were minus the maxilla and mandible. From observations based upon the amount of vertebral "lipping," however, and upon mandibular absorption, it is doubtful that any of these six individuals had reached an age of sixty years.

The mean of the 27 skeletons under twenty-one years of age is 6.5, with a standard error of 1.1. The ages of 13 males and of 13 females were averaged; the undefinable adult was about forty years of age at the time of death. The female average is 42.8, with a standard error of .33. Surprisingly enough, the males averaged a slightly higher mean, 44.3, with a standard error of .44. Neumann reports a similar greater relative male longevity reflected by the skeletons found in the cemetery in White County, Illinois (Neumann and Fowler, 1952:222). The average age at time of death for the Steuben Mound 1 assemblage of 54 skeletons was calculated as being 24.8 years. This is comparable to the Wabash Cemetery assemblage, White County, which was found by Neumann to have been 25.9 years for 25 skeletons. The Wabash Cemetery skeletal assemblage included 14 adults whose mean age at time of death was 43.1 years.

Stature.—There are 25 adults in the Steuben Mound 1 assemblage whose long bones are complete enough for stature computation. Trotter and Gleser (1952:487) found that stature generally has a smaller standard of error when computed from bones of the lower limbs. This suited the Steuben data in that the tibia is the most numerous of the complete long bones. In addition, paired tibiae are the most consistent in length whereas other paired long bones, especially the humerus and the femur, varied from each other in the final computed stature as much as one and one-half inches. Furthermore, it was discovered that, when several long bone lengths of the same individual would correspond to a common stature, the tibia was generally among them.

The "next-best" long bones seemed to be the left radius, the left ulna, the right ulna, the right radius, and the left and right fibula in that order. If the stature computations had been the result of an average of all long bones available, the final individual calculated statures generally would have been about an inch shorter.

The shortest stature computed for the males is 5 feet 4 inches, and the highest is 5 feet 11 inches. Five of the 13 males which could be measured for stature are computed as 5 feet 9 inches. The average height of all 13 is 5 feet 7.5 inches, with a standard error of .07. Neumann and Fowler (1952:214) state that 5 feet 7 inches ". . . corresponds to that of the average Hopewellian male."

Long bones representing 12 females were measured for stature calculations. The mean is 5 feet 5 inches, with a standard error of .06. No information could be found concerning the average height of the Hopewell female. One female in the Steuben Mound 1 skeletal assemblage is 5 feet 9 inches in stature; in contrast, the shortest stature calculated is only 5 feet 2 inches. Two females have stature figures of 5 feet 5 inches; there are 5 over that figure and 5 under it.

Pathology.—There are 12 examples of definite bone abnormalities found in the examination of the 58 Mound 1 skeletons from

Steuben (Morse and Dickson, 1956). Ten are classified as acquired pathology and two are probably of congenital origin. These 12 examples are discussed in the order of their burial number.

The left femur of Burial 13 exhibits a bony spur on the posterior-medial surface of the distal end (Pl. XXVII, Fig. 2). This appears to be an ossification of a ligament where it was attached to the bone. Both femurs are slightly bowed outward in Burial 14, a male over fifty years of age. This is suggestive of the existence of a nutritional disturbance, in youth, possibly rickets. The right humerus of Burial 16 is deformed as a result of a greenstick fracture (Pl. XXVIII, Fig. 1). The second and third thoracic vertebrae of Burial 24 are fused (Pl. XXVIII, Fig. 2, right). The smooth appearance of the fused parts, no apparent evidence of trauma, and the absence of arthritis indicate a congenital origin.

There is a bony growth on the distal end of the first metatarsal of Burial 35. A microscopic section taken through this growth shows a thinning to absence of the articular cartilage (Pl. XXIX, Fig. 1, A - A') and ossification into the under surface of the cartilaginous plate (Pl. XXIX, Fig. 1, B). From a study of both the gross and microscopic specimens, the impression is that this is a degenerative or osteoarthritis condition, probably due to trauma.

The twelfth thoracic and the first lumbar vertebrae of Burial 37 are ankylosed (Pl. XXVIII, Fig. 2, left). The appearance is that of a healed compression fracture. Burial 43 shows a fusion of the left patella and femur; this is believed to have been caused by arthritis.

In Burial 45 the right femur shows the following abnormalities: (1) a shorter neck; (2) a definite twist to the entire bone suggesting a "knock-knee" condition; and, (3) a decrease of by at least one-half of the normal 130 degree angle which the neck of the femur makes with the shaft. Since there are no fracture lines visible, it would be a fair assumption that this was a congenital dislocation.

The skull, including the lower jaw, of Burial 49 is a puzzle (Pl. XXXI, Fig. 2). Several pathologists saw this specimen and could not agree on the diagnosis. This was a bundle burial and, unfortunately, all the bones were not present. There is a marked atrophy of the right side of the lower jaw and of the right zygomatic arch (the upper jaw is missing). In addition there is a deep, rounded depression, about one inch in diameter, located on the internal surface of the skull at the anterior-superior angle of the left parietal bone. The depression is immediately posterior to the coronal suture and lateral to the sagittal suture. Externally, a very small prominence which is hardly noticeable is seen directly above the internal depression. Both the internal and external surfaces of this prominence appear intact with no evidence of fracture or bone erosion. The possibilities are a tumor or blood clot on the surface of the brain which pushed the bone outward without causing erosion, or a skull fracture which healed without leaving any telltale evidence. In either case, unilateral atrophy of the jaw must have been caused by injury to the fifth nerve, either at its origin or along its course.

The right tibia of Burial 56 is thickened and its surface is roughened (Pl. XXIX, Fig. 2, Pl. XXX, Figs. 1 and 2). The bone was sawed longitudinally and a microscopic section was taken through the thickened portion. The sawing was very difficult because of increased bone density. The microscopic section shows a marked increase in the density of the cortical bone (Pl. XXX, Fig. 2). The entire picture is undoubtedly that of a reaction to trauma rather than to infection. In Burial 57, a child of five or six years, the right side of the skull was flattened and twisted. Examination of this specimen revealed that this deformity occurred before death, but as yet no one has ventured a diagnosis.

In considering the abnormalities of the teeth, the condition known as attrition was universal in the adults, becoming quite pronounced as age increased. It might be significant to note that the middle-aged females usually exhibited a more pronounced condition of attrition than did the males of the same age group. Many of the teeth observed have pinpoint cavities and some have larger cavities. Those individuals past forty or fifty had lost some, or all, of their molars and/or premolars. There were no individuals who had lost all their teeth.

One cause of death could be diagnosed correctly. This concerned a female (Burial 6) whose pelvis contained an infant (Burial 7) in breech position. The multiple burial in Pit C and some of the disarticulated skeletons causes one to suspect the possibility of violent death.

Some pathological conditions existing in the mound can be strongly suspected because of a combination of circumstances. For instance, over 40 per cent of the burials found in Mound 1 were those of young children. Up to very recent years the greatest cause of infant mortality was gastro-intestinal disease, usually termed diarrhea of children. These diseases are thought to have been the direct result of poor sanitary conditions, and with the improvement in the sanitary conditions there has been a corresponding decrease in infant and child mortality. The nearby village site is almost nothing but a deep layer of refuse material. Remains of fish, animals, and other debris had been scattered haphazardly, it would seem, over the terrain, undoubtedly resulting in an unsanitary environment which could explain the high incidence of child mortality.

Artificial Cranial Deformation.—With the exceptions of Pits A and B, the incidence of simple occipital deformation (also known as "cradle-board" deformation) appears to be randomly distributed as concerns burial position within Mound 1. Three of four skulls in Pit A and both skulls of the articulated occupants of Pit B exhibit this condition. None of the four skeletons in Pit C and one of the two articulated skeletons in Pit D exhibit simple occipital deformation. This condition exists amongst about half of the other skeletons in Mound 1.

An interpretation of this data hinges, among other factors, upon whether Mound 1 as a whole is the smallest temporal and archaeological unit which can be treated effectively. Pits A and B together form a unit by virtue of being the only two subfloor pits enclosed by their common primary mound. Artifacts were associated only with Pit B, and the three vessels found "probably" represent the earliest artifacts present in the mound. However, heirlooms and/or chance, if operating here, would be powerful factors. Other factors to be considered are involved in what this cranial deformity means in Illinois Valley Hopewell. Is occipital deformation due to individuals being singled out for certain status roles at a very early age through a sort of inheritance of redistributional functions (Chieftainship)? Or is it possibly a means of establishing ethnic differences between societies in geographical proximity? Both are logical interpretations of available data and both can occur on a Hopewell level of cultural development. The main difficulty is that no Hopewell skeletal assemblage has yet been consistent to the extent that either of these interpretations is made probable.

Simple occipital deformation has been said to be a mark of the "higher class" or status group during Hopewell times: "Judging from the whole complex of traits, it is quite evident that the cemetery was one of the common people in contrast to that of members of the priestly or ruling class buried in the elaborate tombs of the mounds. In this connection it is significant that, with perhaps one exception, none of the skulls from the cemetery exhibit artificial cranial deformation. In the mounds many show deformation of the simple occipital type. . . ." (Neumann and Fowler, 1952:222). Neumann and Fowler assume that the mounds and the cemetery belong to the same component, but there is not definite evidence one way or the other. For instance, evidence against such an interpretation is the lack of *Anculosa* beads associated with mound burials though such beads are common artifacts in the cemetery. In the central and southern Illinois Valley, certain types of *Anculosa* beads appear to be associated mainly with Late Hopewell and Jersey Bluff mound burials.

SUMMARY AND INTERPRETATIONS

In the Introduction, five basic premises were stated which were designed to show that we are merely dealing with a normal cultural situation. These premises are that: artifacts and cultures are susceptible to typological treatment; archaeological assemblages are samples; any given site probably is multicomponent; primitive groups are rarely stationary for a long period of time at a single site; and, one part of a primitive community will reflect data very similar to another part of the same community. An understanding of all five is necessary to follow the descriptions and interpretations presented here.

The Steuben Site

The Steuben site, Sections 34 and 35, Steuben Township, Marshall County, Illinois, consists of nine burial mounds on the summits of two neighboring bluffs and a village area which is nine acres in extent and situated between the two bluffs and the Illinois River. Artifact-bearing soil in the village area had originally eroded from the bluff summits. Erosion from the bluffs, and subsequent deposition on the village, apparently took place mainly during the two major aboriginal occupations at Steuben, and was extensive enough to cause an unnamed creek to change its course slightly. The soil, Worthen fine sandy loam, bluff wash, is favorable for agriculture, and the area was productive enough for hunting, fishing, and gathering to supplement an agricultural economy (Appendixes 1-5).

A total of five excavation units, consisting of from two to seven levels each were dug in the Steuben village. A statistical examination of the vertical distribution of pottery in these units indicated that Test Pits I and III are good archaeological samples, whereas the other units seem to be disturbed to the extent of being practically worthless as samples. Furthermore, it is inferred that these two test pits do not represent samples of the same cultural component at the Steuben site, though both seem to be Late Hopewell, that is, both contain a greater proportion of Weaver than Hopewell ware. The component represented by Test Pit III is probably the older of the two. Weaver ware is very much secondary to Havana ware in Test Pit III; in Test Pit I, on the other hand, the relative proportions of these two major wares are reversed. Other striking differences which emphasize the relative dating of these two components include the absence of a number of Havana and Hopewell pottery types found in Test Pit III, and the rarity of such Test Pit III traits as split turkey tarsometatarsus awls and Hopewell flint blades in Test Pit I (Table XVIII, p. 99).

In the other three excavation units, the percentages of sherd types either change significantly by level with no over-all single trend, or are almost evenly mixed so as to appear more homogeneous through time than would be expected for normal culture trait change. It is not to be inferred from this, however, that the two test pits selected as representative samples are completely undisturbed units. Feature 2 in Test Pit I and the cache of four bear canines in Test Pit III demonstrate the presence of minor mixture, and also suggest the possibility of other pits which may have escaped recognition. In addition, the lowest foot of Test Pit I, in which the bed of gravel (Feature 1) was located, probably includes some material represented by the Test Pit III component. But it is assumed that this disturbance is very minor. Both Test Pit II and its extension are mixed to the extent that they may be situated where the two major component's village areas overlap, while Burial 3 appears to have been made by the Test Pit I component into an area which had been occupied by the Test Pit III component.

Hence, there is actually very little data with which to interpret the Steuben site. We feel, however, that as much as possible must be made of the existing data since there is no prospect for further excavation at the Steuben site in the foreseeable future. There are several interpretations possible from the available data, but that of two Late Hopewell components is the one accepted here since it best fits all of the data. Other possible interpretations would be viewing the two components respectively as Middle Hopewell and as Weaver, and/or assuming that these two test pits represent the opposite ends of a continuous occupation of one single component. Also, it might be assumed that several Middle and Late Hopewell and Weaver components are present.

Test Pits I and III, however, indicate that the site was probably uninhabited during the period of time represented by the break between the two components. The bottom foot of Test Pit I seems to include artifacts from both components and hence supports such a break. Also, where artifacts are found together which are thought to be from both components, evidence of interlarding is present. In other words, such an assumed break in occupation is supported by the absence of assemblages which would logically belong within such an occupation break. On the other hand, a shifting village might produce much the same sort of data. Be that as it may, the break seems to be of such magnitude that it would have equaled one or two of the time periods represented by either of the two components. Both components logically would have occupied Steuben for the same approximate length of time. The same biological continuum is probably represented by the two components, assuming that an ethnic group was moving around within a defined territory.

A total of five surface collections from the Steuben village were examined: Schoenbeck, Chase, Elliot, Morse, and the University of Michigan Museum of Anthropology. None of these collections are random, but it is assumed that the UMMA collection is more random than any of the other four. By a comparison with the two main Steuben components, the primary danger of the utilization of a surface collection to attempt archaeological interpretation emerges. The two major Steuben components are not equally represented by the UMMA surface collection. Since part of the area occupied by the youngest component is not available for a surface survey, the multicomponent surface collection was weighted in favor of the oldest component. Such a danger as seems to exist at Steuben probably could be greatly avoided by a controlled surface collection; that is, if different sections of a site were collected from as distinct units, it might be possible to get general indications of the nature of the multicomponentcy which exists.

A consideration of surface collections other than the Morse and UMMA ones has enriched the total Steuben assemblage both by trait duplication and by the addition of new traits. New traits are important because they can indicate the probability of additional components and hence a reconsideration of the possible assemblage membership of other traits which may seem out of place. Also, many new traits may be new merely because of their relative rarity. And many times, rare traits are very important in archaeological interpretation.

TABLE XVIII

TRAIT LIST FOR MAJOR ARCHAEOLOGICAL ASSEMBLAGES FROM THE STEUBEN SITE

	Village Excavations							Village Surface Collections					
Traits	Test Pit I	Test Pit II	Test Pit II Extension (incl. features)	Test Pit III	Test Pit III Extension Upper Level	Test Pit III Extension Lower Level	Mound 1 Excavations	Umma	Schoenbeck	Morse	Chase	Elliot	Other
Havana ware	X	X	X	X	X	X	X	X	X	X	X	X	
Havana ware decreasing in popularity	X			X	NA	NA	NA	NA	NA	NA	NA	NA	NA
Havana ware constitutes between ca. 62 and 85 per cent of total sherds				X			NA		X	X			
Havana ware constitutes between ca. 3 and 25 per cent of total sherds	X						NA				X	X	
Havana ware constitutes more than 85 per cent of total sherds						X	NA						
Havana Cordmarked	X	X	X	X	X	X		X	X	X	X	X	
Havana Plain	X	X	X	X	X	X		X	X	X	X	X	
Havana Plain to Havana Cordmarked ratio about equal	X						NA	X					
Havana Cordmarked Prominent over Havana Plain		X	X	X	X	X	NA		X		X	X	
Steuben Punctated	X	X	X	X	X	X	X	X	X	X	X	X	
Steuben Punctated increasing in popularity				X	NA	NA	NA	NA	NA	NA	NA	NA	NA
Steuben Punctated decreasing in popularity	X				NA	NA	NA	NA	NA	NA	NA	NA	NA
Naples Dentate Stamped, Steuben variety	X	X	X	X	X			X	X	X	X	X	
Hummel Dentate Stamped, Steuben variety	X	X	X	X	X	X		X	X	X	X	X	
Hummel Plain Stamped									X				
Naples Barred Ovoid Stamped										X			
Neteler Dentate Crescent Stamped									X	X			
Havana Zoned Incised			X	X					X				
Havana Zoned Dentate Stamped		X	X	X					X			X	
Havana Zoned Plain Rocked Stamped			X	X									
Havana Zoned Punctated				X									
Havana Dentate Rocked Stamped				X							X		
Havana Plain Rocked Stamped					X	X					X		
Havana Random Punctated		X											
Victory Brushed		X							X	X	X		
Havana Miscellaneous Incised								X	X	X			
Havana Crosshatched Rim										X			
Weaver ware	X	X	X	X	X		X	X	X	X	X	X	
Weaver ware increasing in popularity	X		X	X	NA	NA	NA	NA	NA	NA	NA	NA	NA
Weaver ware constitutes between ca. 75 and 97 per cent of total sherds	X						NA						
Weaver ware constitutes between ca. 13 and 35 per cent of total sherds				X			NA		X	X			

TABLE XVIII (Cont.)

Traits	Village Excavations							Village Surface Collections					
	Test Pit I	Test Pit II	Test Pit II Extension (incl. features)	Test Pit III	Test Pit III Extension Upper Level	Test Pit III Extension Lower Level	Mound 1 Excavations	Umma	Schoenbeck	Morse	Chase	Elliot	Other
Weaver ware constitutes less than ca. 13 per cent of total sherds.						X	NA				X	X	
Weaver Cordmarked	X	X	X	X	X		X	X	X	X	X	X	
Weaver Plain.	X	X	X	X	X			X	X	X	X	X	
Weaver Cordmarked prominent over Weaver Plain. . . .			X	X	X	NA	NA	X	X	X	X	X	
Weaver Plain prominent over Weaver Cordmarked	X	X				NA	NA						
Weaver Notched or Wavy Lip .	X	X	X	X			X	X		X	X		
Weaver Plain Stamped.	X									X			
Weaver Cord-Wrapped Stick Stamped.								X		X			
Weaver Incised		X						X		X	X		
Weaver Punctated Lip.		X									X		
Weaver Miscellaneous Punctated		X									X		
Weaver Miscellaneous Incised.											X		
Weaver Other.				X				X					
Hopewell Ware.	X	X	X	X	X	X	X	X	X	X		X	
Hopewell Rim	X	X	X	X			X	X	X	X		X	
Hopewell Plain.		X	X	X			X	X	X	X			
Hopewell Zoned Incised.	X	X	X	X	X		X	X	X	X			
Hopewell Zoned Red Filmed. .								X					
Hopewell Zoned Brushed									X				
Hopewell Zoned Dentate Stamped		X	X						X				
Hopewell Zoned Dentate Rocked Stamped	X	X	X	X		X		X		X			
Hopewell Zoned Plain Rocked Stamped			X	X			X		X				
Hopewell Zoned Cord-Wrapped Stick			X										
Hopewell Plain Rocked Stamped.				X	X		X	X	X	X		X	
Hopewell Dentate Rocked Stamped						X		X		X			
Hopewell Red Filmed		X	X		X							X	
Hopewell Brushed												X	
Brangenburg Plain								X	X				
Montezuma Punctated		X							X			X	
Baehr Brushed.	X	X	X		X			X	X	X		X	
Baehr Zoned Brushed							X		X	X			
Baehr Zoned Punctated									X				
Baehr Dentate Rocked Stamped									X				
Baehr Plain Rocked Stamped .									X				
Baehr Plain									X				
Baehr Incised									X				
Blumenshein Cord Impressed.									X				
Mossville Cordmarked									X				
Cahokia Cordmarked.									X			X	
Irregular shaped lump of clay			X					X		X			

TABLE XVIII (Cont.)

Traits	Village Excavations							Village Surface Collections					
	Test Pit I	Test Pit II	Test Pit II Extension (incl. features)	Test Pit III	Test Pit III Extension Upper Level	Test Pit III Extension Lower Level	Mound 1 Excavations	Umma	Schoenbeck	Morse	Chase	Elliot	Other
Snyders Corner Notched				X			X	X		X	X	X	
Marshall Barbed, variety fine	X	X	X		X			X		X	X	X	
Marshall Barbed, variety rugged										X	X	X	
Marshall Barbed, variety crude										X		X	
Steuben Expanded Stemmed, variety long and slender	X	X	X					X		X	X	X	
Steuben Expanded Stemmed, variety squat and thick								X		X	X	X	
Steuben Expanded Stemmed, variety small and thin		X								X	X	X	
Large Side Notched, variety straight and concave base		X								X	X	X	
Large Side Notched, variety convex base								X		X	X	X	
Contracting and Straight Stemmed, variety pointed base			X							X		X	
Contracting and Straight Stemmed, variety rounded base			X							X	X	X	
Contracting and Straight Stemmed, variety straight base	X							X		X	X	X	
Small Triangular				X	X			X		X	X	X	
Triangular knife	X	X						X		X	X	X	
Ribbon Flake knife, variety used	X	X	X	X				X		X	X	X	
Ribbon Flake knife, variety worked on one edge	X	X		X				X		X	X	X	
Ribbon Flake knife, variety worked on both edges	X	X	X	X				X		X	X	X	
Ribbon Flake to total flint ratio greater than 1:5				X									
Free Flake scraper, variety used	X	X	X	X	X			X		X			
Free Flake scraper, variety slightly worked		X	X	X	X			X		X	X	X	
Free Flake scraper, variety worked on all edges	X		X					X		X	X	X	
Unused Free Flakes	X	X	X	X	X		X	X		X			
Free Flake end scraper				X				X		X	X	X	
Ribbon Flake end scraper								X		X	X	X	
Free Flake scraper with concave edge	X	X		X	X			X		X			
Ribbon Flake scraper with concave edge				X				X		X		X	
Plano-Convex scraper					X			X		X	X	X	
Bifaced scraper			X	X	X		X	X		X		X	
Graver made on free flake				X				X		X			
Graver made on ribbon flake								X					
Flint Hammerstone and/or core	X	X	X	X	X			X		X			

TABLE XVIII (Cont.)

	Village Excavations							Village Surface Collections					
Traits	Test Pit I	Test Pit II	Test Pit II Extension (incl. features)	Test Pit III	Test Pit III Extension Upper Level	Test Pit III Extension Lower Level	Mound 1 Excavations	Umma	Schoenbeck	Morse	Chase	Elliot	Other
Flint effigy									X*	X		X	
Flint marble									X				
Grooved-stone axe, unknown variety													X*
Stone celt, variety rectangular										X	X	X	
Stone celt, variety rectangular with flaring bit . . .										X	X		
Stone celt, variety round										X			
Stone gorget, variety rectangular										X			
Stone gorget, variety oval . . .									X	X			
Stone gorget, variety reel-shaped										X			
Stone gorget, unclassifiable variety										X		X	
Stone hammerstone, including chips	X	X	X	X	X			X	X	X	X		
Grooved-stone hammerstone, maul, or net weight. .									X	X	X		
Retouched large granite flake.												X	
Sandstone abrader, variety grooved.					X							X	
Quartzite abrader, variety grooved.											X		
Granite discoidal, variety biconcave with rounded cup edge												X	
Limestone plummet, variety teardrop-shaped and grooved												X	
Human head effigy of argillaceous sandstone									X				
Small triangular-shaped mica sheet											X		
Rubbed hematite												X	
Chipped hematite bifaced artifact												X	
Hematite gorget, variety rectangular											X		
Copper fragment or sheet . . .							X			X			
Copper cylinder with perforations		X											
Copper awl or drifter, Wilson variety										X			
Galena with abraded edges . . .										X			
Waterworn hematite and limonite	X	X	X	X	X								
Deer metatarsal awl, variety intact head										X			
Deer metatarsal awl, variety single-pointed splinter	X	X					X			X			
Deer metatarsal awl, variety double-pointed splinter . . .	X	X								X			
Deer metatarsal awl, unclassifiable variety		X	X							X			

TABLE XVIII (Cont.)

Traits	Village Excavations							Village Surface Collections					
	Test Pit I	Test Pit II	Test Pit II Extension (incl. features)	Test Pit III	Test Pit III Extension Upper Level	Test Pit III Extension Lower Level	Mound 1 Excavations	Umma	Schoenbeck	Morse	Chase	Elliot	Other
Deer ulna awl, unclassifiable variety				X	X					X			
Mammal bone awl, unclassifiable variety	X								X	X	X	X	
Split turkey tarso-metatarsus awl, Hopewell variety				X	X					X			
Bird bone awl, unclassifiable variety	X			X	X					X			
Bird bone awl to total bone awl ratio greater than 1:2 .				X									
Mammal bone scraper or chisel		X										X	
Mammal bone spatula							X						
Polished mammal bone chip. .		X											
Bone punctator, Steuben variety	X	X		X						X			
Game bone, variety notched distal end	X												
Turtle carapace vessel and/or spoon	X	X	X	X	X		X						
Turtle carapace rattle										X			
Perforated black bear canine, variety two complete perforations				X									
Perforated black bear canine, variety two incomplete perforations							X						
Grooved black bear canine . . .							X						
Antler "drifter"										X			
Barbed socketed antler tine . .						X						X	
Unclassifiable antler artifacts	X	X	X	X	X				X	X		X	
Mussel shell hoe, unclassifiable variety	X	X	X	X	X				X	X		X	
Mussel shell hoe, variety unmodified.	X	X	X	X	X		X			X		X	
Mussel shell hoe, variety ground-down hinge	X			X					X*	X		X	
Mussel shell spoon, variety plain handle							X						
Mussel shell spoon, variety notched handle							X						
Mussel shell spoon, unclassifiable variety										X			
Mussel shell scraper		X											
Mussel shell rattle		X											
Conch shell vessel (Busycon perversum)							X						
Small shell disc beads							X						

Symbols: X, present; NA, not applicable; *, hearsay.
Identification of Schoenbeck Pottery by James B. Griffin, Director, UMMA.

Table XIX, p. 106, sums up the probable component membership of Hopewell traits found at Steuben. Some of the surface finds are included in one or both of the two main complexes because of their similarity to excavated artifacts. Some are placed because of evidence from other Hopewell sites since these traits were not found in a relatively tight cultural context at Steuben. Other artifacts are excluded from Table XIX because it is felt that there is sufficient evidence that they do not belong within either of the two Steuben Hopewell components. A comparison of Tables XVIII and XIX will readily reveal which traits were interpreted in one of these three ways.

A minimum of three non-Hopewell assemblages may be inferred. All three, perhaps, can be described as "cultural droppings" or as very small and minor campsite situations. The two Cahokia Cordmarked sherds, one each from the Elliot and Schoenbeck collections, are definitely Middle Mississippi. No other distinctive Middle Mississippi artifacts were found at Steuben with the exception of the Cahokia side-notched projectile point from the Elliot collection (Pl. XIV), and this sherd type is prevalent in the Cahokia area around Late Old Village and possibly Early Trappist times.

One Blumenshein Cord Impressed and eleven Mossville Cordmarked sherds, in the Schoenbeck collection, are sherd types found in Maples Mills. There are apparently two sorts of Maples Mills complexes: one is heavily influenced by Middle Mississippi, as inferred from the presence of vessel handles and by vessel shape and decoration; the other does not seem to have attributes which can be interpreted as direct Mississippi influence. Otherwise, both complexes appear to be very similar though little is known about either. Further, Maples Mills is very similar to what is called Effigy Mound. Probably the two Maples Mills complexes are foci within an Effigy Mound Aspect which in turn has every appearance of belonging in the Late Woodland phase. The 12 Steuben sherds probably belong in the earlier of the two Maples Mills complexes. It is not known how late in time the Late Woodland Weaver Sub-Aspect lasts, but it is known that it existed between the Hopewell and Maples Mills periods. Hence, Maples Mills dates from around the end of the first millenium A.D. The Small Triangular projectile point category may be Maples Mills. Some of the individual points, however, may belong in the Test Pit I complex since there are so many points in proportion to the Maples Mills pottery represented. On the other hand, nowhere has it been demonstrated that such points do belong in a Hopewell context. It is also possible to place the discoidal from the Elliot collection in Maples Mills, but as demonstrated before, this artifact class has been found in Copena and there is some evidence that it may belong in a Late Hopewell context in Illinois as well. Certain Weaver sherds found in the plow zone in the village excavations similarly may be interpreted as belonging in Maples Mills, that is, Weaver Random Punctated and Weaver with Punctated Lip, both from Test Pit II. Weaver Miscellaneous Incised, Chase collection, also may be Maples Mills.

A plummet and two grooved axes plus the absence of any Early Woodland pottery indicate the probability of a preceramic component at the Steuben site. All three artifacts are very commonly found in Late Archaic. Contracting and Straight Stemmed, varieties pointed, rounded, and straight base, are projectile point categories represented in Late Archaic. Also some of the individual points included in the two varieties of Large Side Notched may be Late Archaic, especially the Hemphill-like notched scraper. In addition, the retouched large granite flake may be Late Archaic, as well as the hematite artifacts.

There are nine mounds upon the two bluffs west of the village site. Mound 1 was completely excavated (Pl. XXXI, Fig. 1) and another five near-by mounds on the southern bluff tested by us. All but Mound 1 had been previously excavated, and it is strongly suspected that many, or all, of these five were dug by the Peoria Scientific Association in the fall of 1877. It is not known who dug the three mounds on the northern bluff which exhibit evidence of having been considerably disturbed.

The pit burials were the earliest inhumations made in Mound 1 (Fig. 6). There is no evidence as to which pit is the earliest. Next, burials had been made in the primary mounds over the pits, and the latest inhumations were those above and between the primary mounds. It is possible that the Mound 1 assemblage represents one component though there are some problems to such an interpretation. A total of 15 males, 16 females, 4 unclassified adults, and 23 children under 14 years of age were found in Mound 1. In addition, several other individuals were represented by human bones scattered throughout the fill in the central portions of the mound. The mean age at death of children under 21 was 6.5; that of females was 42.8; that of males was 44.3; and, that of all the skeletons was 24.8. The average height of the males was 5 feet $7\frac{1}{2}$ inches; that of females was 5 feet 5 inches. In the study of the pathology, microscopic sections were made of two specimens. Although these were not of too much help in arriving at a diagnosis, it is suggestive that more study along this line might be of considerable help in analyzing pathological conditions of prehistoric bones.

TABLE XIX

TENTATIVE TRAIT LIST OF THE CREW AND STEUBEN FOCI, ILLINOIS ASPECT, HOPEWELL PHASE, WOODLAND PATTERN

Trait	Crew Focus	Steuben Focus
Havana ware	X	X
Havana ware decreasing in popularity	X	X
Havana ware constitutes between ca. 62 and 85 per cent of total sherds	X	
Havana ware constitutes between ca. 3 and 25 per cent of total sherds		X
Havana Cordmarked	X	X
Havana Plain	X	X
Havana Plain to Havana Cordmarked ratio about equal		X
Havana Cordmarked prominent over Havana Plain	X	
Steuben Punctated	X	X
Steuben Punctated increasing in popularity	X	
Steuben Punctated decreasing in popularity		X
Naples and Hummel Dentate Stamped, Steuben variety	X	X
Hummel Plain Stamped	X	X
Naples Barred Ovoid Stamped	X	
Neteler Dentate Crescent Stamped	X	
Havana Zoned Incised	X	
Havana Zoned Dentate Stamped	X	
Havana Zoned Plain Rocked Stamped	X	
Havana Zoned Punctated	X	
Havana Dentate Rocked Stamped	X	
Havana Plain Rocked Stamped	X	
Havana Random Punctated	X	
Victory Brushed		X
Havana Miscellaneous Incised	X	X
Havana Crosshatched Rim		X
Weaver ware	X	X
Weaver ware increasing in popularity	X	X
Weaver ware constitutes between ca. 75 and 97 per cent of total sherds		X
Weaver ware constitutes between ca. 13 and 35 per cent of total sherds	X	
Weaver Cordmarked	X	X
Weaver Plain	X	X
Weaver Cordmarked prominent over Weaver Plain	X	
Weaver Plain prominent over Weaver Cordmarked		X
Weaver Notched or Wavy Lip	X	X
Weaver Plain Stamped		X
Weaver Cord-Wrapped Stick Stamped	X	X
Weaver Incised	X	
Weaver Other	X	
Hopewell ware	X	X
Hopewell Rim	X	X
Hopewell Plain	X	X
Hopewell Zoned Incised	X	X
Hopewell Zoned Red Filmed		
Hopewell Zoned Brushed	X	X
Hopewell Zoned Dentate Stamped	X	

TABLE XIX (Cont.)

Trait	Crew Focus	Steuben Focus
Hopewell Zoned Dentate Rocked Stamped	X	
Hopewell Zoned Plain Rocked Stamped	X	
Hopewell Zoned Cord-Wrapped Stick	X	
Hopewell Plain Rocked Stamped	X	
Hopewell Dentate Rocked Stamped	X	
Hopewell Red Filmed	X	
Hopewell Brushed		X
Brangenburg Plain	X	
Montezuma Punctated	X	X
Baehr Brushed		X
Baehr Zoned Brushed	X	
Baehr Zoned Punctated	X	
Baehr Dentate Rocked Stamped	X	
Baehr Plain Rocked Stamped	X	
Baehr Plain		X
Baehr Incised	X	X
Snyders Corner Notched	X	
Marshall Barbed, variety fine	?	X
Marshall Barbed, variety rugged		X
Marshall Barbed, variety crude		X
Steuben Expanded Stemmed, variety long and slender	?	X
Steuben Expanded Stemmed, variety squat and thick		X
Steuben Expanded Stemmed, variety small and thin		X
Large Side Notched, variety straight and concave base	X	
Large Side Notched, variety convex base	X	?
Contracting and Straight Stemmed, variety pointed base	X	
Contracting and Straight Stemmed, variety rounded base	X	
Contracting and Straight Stemmed, variety straight base	X	X
Small Triangular		?
Triangular Knife	X	X
Ribbon Flake Knife, variety used	X	X
Ribbon Flake Knife, variety worked on one edge	X	X
Ribbon Flake Knife, variety worked on both edges	X	X
Ribbon Flake to Total Flint ratio greater than 1:5	X	
Free Flake Scraper, variety used	X	X
Free Flake Scraper, variety slightly worked	X	X
Free Flake Scraper, variety worked on all edges	X	X
Free Flake End Scraper	X	
Ribbon Flake end scraper	X	
Free Flake scraper with concave edge	X	X
Ribbon Flake scraper with concave edge	X	
Plano-Convex scraper	X	
Bifaced scraper	X	X
Graver made on free flake	X	X
Graver made on ribbon flake	X	
Flint Hammerstone and/or core	X	X
Flint effigy	X	
Flint marble	X	
Stone celt, variety rectangular	X	X
Stone celt, variety rectangular with flaring bit	X	X

TABLE XIX (Cont.)

Trait	Crew Focus	Steuben Focus
Stone celt, variety round		X̲
Stone gorget, variety rectangular	X̲	X̲
Stone gorget, variety oval	X̲	X̲
Stone gorget, variety reel-shaped		X̲
Stone hammerstone	X	X
Grooved-stone hammerstone, maul, or net weight	X̲	
Sandstone or quartzite abrader, variety grooved		?
Granite discoidal, variety biconcave with rounded cup edge		?
Small stone human head effigy (broken from figurine)	X̲	
Small triangular-shaped mica sheet	X̲	
Rubbed hematite	?	
Chipped hematite bifaced artifact	?	
Hematite gorget, variety rectangular	?	
Copper fragment or sheet	X̲	
Copper cylinder with perforations	X̲	
Copper awl or drifter, Wilson variety	X̲	
Galena with abraded edges	X̲	
Deer metatarsal awl, variety intact head	X̲	X̲
Deer metatarsal awl, variety single-pointed splinter	X̲	X
Deer metatarsal awl, variety double-pointed splinter	X̲	X
Deer ulna awl, unclassifiable variety	X̲	X̲
Split turkey tarso-metatarsus awl, Hopewell variety	X	X̲
Bird bone awl to total bone awl ratio greater than 1:2	X	
Mammal bone scraper or chisel	X̲	X̲
Mammal bone spatula	X	
Polished mammal bone chip	X̲	
Bone punctator, Steuben variety	X	X
Game bone, variety notched distal end		X
Turtle carapace vessel and/or spoon	X	X
Turtle carapace rattle	X̲	
Perforated black bear canine, variety two complete perforations	X	
Perforated black bear canine, variety two incomplete perforations	X	
Grooved black bear canine	X	
Antler "drifter"	X̲	
Barbed socketed antler tine	X	
Mussel shell hoe, variety unmodified	X	X
Mussel shell hoe, variety ground-down hinge	X	X
Mussel shell spoon, variety plain handle	X	X̲
Mussel shell spoon, variety notched handle	X	
Mussel shell scraper	X̲	X̲
Mussel shell rattle	X̲	X̲
Conch shell vessel (*Busycon perversum*)	X	
Small shell disc beads	X	

X signifies that evidence for focus placement is based on the Steuben site excavations and X̲ that placement is based on other evidence.

By and large, the artifacts found in Mound 1 are those described for the earliest Hopewell component at Steuben (Tables XVIII, XIX). But the main difficulties here are the rarity of artifacts present in Mound 1 and the unknown degree of probability that Mound 1 is one archaeological unit and not two. The high incidence of Simple Occipital Deformation in two of the four burial pits may mean very little since the reason for Simple Occipital Deformation is not known definitely. The large number of burials within one mound is characteristic of Late Hopewell as is the relatively large proportion of children.

Artifacts in the Mound fill were scarce and consisted only of a Snyders Corner Notched knife, some Weaver Cordmarked and Steuben Punctated sherds, and a few flint chips, animal bones, and shell hoes. If Mound 1 were to be linked with the latest Steuben Hopewell component, there is the difficulty of only one Weaver vessel being present, and this vessel conceivably could have been intrusive into the mound. There is a shift from round to oval mounds during or at the end of Late Hopewell in the Illinois Valley. This shift is even traceable, for instance, in Jo Daviess County, Illinois, where there is a transition from Hopewell into Effigy Mound (Bennett, 1945). The internal constitution of mounds 7, 8, and 9 is not known, but externally they are oval in shape. Mound 1 began as a series of round mounds and the near-by five mounds are all round. In Mound 1 were found small and shallow central subfloor burial pits under primary mounds otherwise essentially sterile of burials except near the pits themselves, a possible roofed log tomb, artificial subsoil floors around and between burial pits, and a central alignment of burials. All of these indicate that Mound 1 belongs with the earliest Steuben Hopewell component since they are Middle Hopewell traits. However, burial customs are apparently among those cultural traits which are the slowest to change (Wray and Schoff, 1953).

Unfortunately, burial practices among contemporary primitive peoples are not well enough described in the literature to tell if it is normal to not bury in an ancestral mound. Usually when multicomponent mounds occur archaeologically, the multicomponentcy is evident because of a lot of differences and it may be argued that the mounds were not considered strictly ancestral by the later groups utilizing them. In certain Ohio Hopewell and Middle Mississippi mounds, there is ample evidence of a long period of selective burying but these mounds apparently are situated at fairly stable ceremonial centers.

In the Pike and Fulton County, Illinois, area, there seems to be a characteristic burial mound pattern in Middle Hopewell.

Large rectangular subfloor tombs are made of up to three large logs placed horizontally on top of each other at each side and a log roof constructed over this. The logs usually are chinked with clay and have a mat covering extending onto the floor from the surface of the mound supporting the logs on the side, being kept in place with split elk longbone pins. The subfloor pit usually is shallow, normally around ten inches below the subsoil surface, but the tomb itself may be five or more feet high. Sometimes, a mat on top of the log roof was kept in place by rocks. Primarily it seems, the tombs functioned as structures where the dead were prepared for burial in near-by small and deep, small and shallow, or large and shallow, rectangular pits roofed with logs resting on horizontal logs placed just inside or outside the pit (Cole and Deuel, 1937; personal communications, Gregory Perino; and personal experience).

There are log tombs present at Dickison (Walker, 1952), and there is some evidence for them in the Goodall focus in Michigan (Quimby, 1941). Classic log tombs have been reported from Jo Daviess County (Bennett, 1945), and in Wisconsin (McKern, 1931; and Cooper, 1933). Conversely, stone slabs are found in place of logs in many mounds attributed to later Late Hopewell complexes in the Illinois Valley, and the stone slab or crypt burial seems to be a wide-spread Late Hopewell and Early Late Woodland trait. At Steuben, three of the burial pits seemed to be merely pits, and the included skeletons which were probably wrapped in matting had had pit fill distributed directly upon them before the construction of the primary mounds.

The probability is that any artifact found at Steuben will belong to one or another, or both Hopewell components. Table XIX is the tentative trait listing for each of the two major components at Steuben. Many of the traits are placed on the list according to their provenience in the village excavations. Others are placed either because of their similarity to traits whose placements are supported by evidence derived from the excavations, or because of their apparent degree of similarity to traits which are considered as classic Hopewell. In explanation of this latter criteria, the two components are respectively early and late within Late Hopewell and it is assumed that these traits are historically related to traits associated with Middle Hopewell. Hence, the farther removed in time, the more dissimilar traits in Middle and Late Hopewell should be. All trait lists are tentative, and the two presented here may be more tentative than usual because of the small scale of excavation carried on.

Traits such as "site near river," "burial mounds," "pottery," and "projectile points" were not included because of their extreme generality and because both components obviously contain such traits. It may be worthwhile, however, to include some of these in a revised trait list. Comparative trait lists of other sites are not included. The absence of a trait in both Steuben components, with the exception of extremely general traits common to both, is shown by the absence of that trait in the table.

Late Hopewell, in general, represents a gradual degeneration of culture, reflected by the loss of many of the more exotic and elaborate traits present in Middle Hopewell. The number of pottery types decreases, culminating in some Late Woodland sites in Illinois which have only Canteen or Weaver Cordmarked and Plain types, often found on the same vessel. Log tombs with their many elaborate grave goods disappear. More individuals are buried in the same mound. Steuben Punctated pottery appears, but many Hopewell and Havana types disappear and are not replaced by new additions. The flint-working techniques are not as precise or varied. Such artifacts as effigy curved-based platform pipes, grizzly bear teeth, obsidian, and copper sheets, celts, and earspools are not present. More pottery vessels are found with burials than are found in Middle Hopewell. Pottery, refreshingly enough, is on the whole better made, and Weaver Ware appears to represent a sort of technological improvement. The cultural degeneration, or loss of archaeologically observable traits, is startling. This is all we can offer at the present time though many speculative causes can be put forth, that is, climatic change, population explosion, epidemics, delayed sociological adjustment, and others. This sort of speculation, however, will have to await good archaeological descriptions of Middle Hopewell and Late Woodland components. The Steuben site is a beginning toward pinpointing the above-mentioned degeneration of culture during Late Hopewell.

Classification within Hopewell

It has been demonstrated that there are at least two Hopewell components at the Steuben site. Throughout this paper both have been referred to as "Late Hopewell," being differentiated from "Early" and "Middle Hopewell." This is one way of classifying the two Steuben Hopewell components, but it still tells very little about these two components and their relationships within Hopewell in general. The McKern Taxonomic System was developed to fill such a need (Guthe, 1937; Griffin, 1943). Unfortunately, very little has been attempted, at least in Illinois, regarding the utilization of this taxonomic system. The main difficulty would seem to be that its utilization entails a great deal of seemingly tedious work.

A beginning at using the McKern Taxonomic System in Illinois Hopewell was made in *Rediscovering Illinois* (Cole and Deuel, 1937). In that publication, the Ogden-Fettie focus was named. Unfortunately, Ogden-Fettie was poorly defined, and oddly enough resulted in merely including most or all of the Fulton County Hopewell sites. Since 1937, the conclusions of Illinois Hopewell papers have merely stated that the concerned site is Hopewell or related to the so-called Ogden-Fettie focus. By and large, the data presented in these papers have not been comprehensive enough for use in applying the McKern Taxonomic System.

Table XIX is a summary of the traits of the two Hopewell components at Steuben. The two components are significantly different, but at the same time both have many traits in common. As mentioned before, there is a great deal of difficulty in comparing either to previously published data. Therefore it is unnecessary to discuss the results of such a survey of the literature, mainly because it was unprofitable since many of the traits discussed here have not been discussed elsewhere. Unrewarding as it was, however, the survey did not reveal the published existence of definable components like either of the two Steuben components. A component is a combination of essentially identical archaeological assemblages from a single site, which have the basic attributes of good representative samples. Similar components make up a focus which is a minimal culture type. At Steuben, the two components are significantly different in type and hence are considered to belong within different foci. At this time, each seems to be the only sample of their respective foci. The latest component is named the Steuben focus, and the earliest the Crew focus. The former name comes from the name of the type site, and the latter from the Christian name of the owner of the type site. Table XIX compares the two foci.

The name "Hopewell" first was used by Mills to designate mound finds similar to those found in the Hopewell group in southern Ohio (Mills, 1906:135). Although Cyrus Thomas had described Hopewell-like finds from Wisconsin in 1894, Hopewell was not widely recognized as existing outside southern Ohio until 1927 (McKern, 1931:195-96). Since around 1940, Hopewell has been generally recognized as being present throughout much of the Eastern United States.

A number of sites in Illinois and neighboring states seem to cluster together in type and may belong in the Illinois Aspect (Baker and others, 1941; Powell, 1957; Griffin, 1941; Cole and Deuel, 1937; Deuel, 1952; Bennett, 1945; McKern, 1931; Cooper, 1933; Wilford, 1955; Wedel, 1943; Schultz and Spaulding, 1948; Griffin, 1946; Quimby, 1941; McGregor, 1958). The old "Elemental Aspect" included foci in the Illinois and Ohio Aspects, and thus has been revised (Guthe, 1937:69-70). The Illinois, Ohio, and Southern Aspects cluster together to make up the Hopewell Phase, and this latter culture type in turn is a component of the Woodland Pattern.

Radiocarbon Dates

In addition to the two mentioned in the Physical Environment section of this paper, there are six radiocarbon dates, made on six separate samples, from the Steuben site. Two samples are from each of the three most important archaeological units: Mound 1, Test Pit I, and Test Pit III. Unfortunately, these dates do little more than support the relative dating of the Crew and Steuben foci, and do not lend any support concerning the probable focus membership for Mound 1.

Two samples, M-545 and M-548, were made up respectively of bits of charcoal collected in the 1-1.5 and 2-2.5 foot levels of Test Pit III. The charcoal occurred as fragments within most of each level. Sample M-545 dated at 1900 ± 200 years ago, and M-548 dated at 2010 ± 200 years ago. In terms of the Christian calendar, these samples date from around the first and second centuries immediately before and after Christ. Assuming that Test Pit III is a cross section of the whole of the Crew focus occupation at the Steuben site, then these samples probably date the early and middle periods of the occupation. From a consideration of other Illinois Hopewell dates (Griffin, 1958), the upper limits of the standard deviation of the two dates probably are closest to the true dating of the Crew focus. In other words, the Crew focus probably dates from around the turn of the second century A.D.

In Test Pit I, two charcoal samples, M-440 and M-441, were also collected. Each sample respectively was collected from charcoal concentrations in the 2-2.5 and 2.5-3 foot levels. Sample M-440 dated at 1325 ± 200 years ago, and M-441 dated at 1275 ± 200 years ago. These two samples, then, date from around the fourth through eighth centuries A.D. They probably date the early and middle periods of the Steuben focus occupation at the Steuben site. Probably, the true date is near the earliest limits of the standard deviation; that is, around the fifth century A.D. It is interesting to note, however, that Carbon-14 dates on Late Woodland samples have tended so far to cluster within a post A.D. 700 time period (Griffin, 1958). But a minimum terminal date for Hopewell in Illinois of A.D. 500 is generally accepted by most interested archaeologists.

The final two Steuben samples were collected in Mound 1. Sample M-378 dated at 1660 ± 250 years ago (Griffin, 1958:14). This sample consisted of charcoal taken from a burnt log which was lying beside Burial 43 near the edge of Pit D in Mound 1 (Pl. XXII, Fig. 2). Fragments from the burnt skull of Burial 43, Mound 1, made up Sample M-380, and dated at 1650 ± 250 years ago (Griffin, 1958:14). Plotted against the Christian calendar, these samples date from around the first through the fifth centuries A.D., thus overlapping in time with the first standard deviations of the Crew and Steuben foci dates. Artifacts found in this general area in Mound 1 were a broken deer bone awl in Pit D, and the burial associations of Numbers 39-41 were a conch shell vessel, a mussel and a turtle shell spoon, a mammal bone spatula, and a Hopewell Plain Rocked Stamped vessel. Burials Numbers 39-41 are later in time than Burial 43, but it is not known how much later. The radiocarbon samples seem to be associated with an earlier mound construction stage since they were within the primary mound. The rocked stamped vessel referred to here exhibits the wide-spaced rocked imprints usually attributed to Late Hopewell (Griffin, 1952:120); but, how early or late it begins is not known. Mound 1 has been tentatively put into the Crew focus, and for this reason the earlier limits of the first standard deviations probably are closest to a true date for the two Mound 1 samples.

APPENDIX A

FAUNA FROM TEST PIT I BY LEVELS

Identifier: Paul W. Parmalee, Curator of Zoology, Illinois State Museum, Springfield

Level	Common Name	Species	Specimens
1	Blue point	*Amblema peruviana*	3 valves
1	Spike	*Elliptio dilatatus*	4 valves
1	Fat mucket	*Lampsilis siliquoidea*	1 valve
1	Unidentifiable mussel shell fragments		4 valves
1	White-tailed deer	*Odocoileus virginianus*	1 calcaneun 1 tarsus 1 metatarsus
1	Freshwater drum	*Aplodinotus grunniens*	3 otoliths
1	Fish	sp.?	1 vertebra fragment
1	Pond terrapin	*Pseudemys* sp., probably *P. scripta*	1 femur fragment
1	Unidentifiable bone fragments; most are large mammals and probably deer		28 bones
2	Mucket	*Actinonaias carinata*	3 valves
2	Blue point	*Amblema peruviana*	2 valves
2	Washboard	*Megalonaias gigantea*	1 valve
2	Spike	*Elliptio dilatatus*	7 valves
2	Fat mucket	*Lampsilis siliquoidea*	1 valve
2	Yellow sand-shell (possibly slough)	*Lampsilis anodontoides* (possibly *L. fallaciosa)*	1 valve
2	Unidentifiable mussel shell fragments		27 valves
2	White-tailed deer	*Odocoileus virginianus*	2 calcaneae 1 tarsus 2 phalanges
2	Canid	*Canis* sp.	1 humerus fragment
2	Fish	sp.?	3 dentary and other fragments
2	Small bird	sp.?	2 bone fragments
2	Pond terrapin and/ or painted turtle	*Pseudemys scripta* and/ or *Chrysemys picta*	1 carapace fragment
2	Unidentifiable fragments; most are large mammal and probably deer		88 bones
3	Butterfly	*Plagiola lineolata*	1 valve
3	Washboard	*Megalonaias gigantea*	1 valve
3	Pocketbook	*Lampsilis ventricosa*	1 valve
3	Pigtoe	*Fusconaia undata*	1 valve
3	Pimple-back	*Quadrula pustulosa*	1 valve
3	Blue point	*Amblema peruviana*	14 valves
3	Spike	*Elliptio dilatatus*	19 valves
3	Small niggerhead	*Pleurobema cordatum*	1 valve
3	Niggerhead	*Fusconaia ebenus*	1 valve
3	Pink heel-splitter	*Proptera alata*	2 valves
3	Mucket	*Actinonaias carinata*	3 valves
3	Fat mucket	*Lampsilis siliquoidea*	5 valves

Level	Common Name	Species	Specimens
3	Slough sand-shell	*Lampsilis fallaciosa*	1 valve
3	Unidentifiable mussel shell fragments		23 valves
3	White-tailed deer	*Odocoileus virginianus*	2 antler fragments
			2 scapulae
			3 dentary
			3 ulnae
			2 radii
			2 phalanges
			1 rib
			1 tibia
			1 metatarsus
			1 calcaneus
			2 tarsi
			2 vertebrae
3	Pond terrapin and/ or painted turtle	*Pseudemys scripta* and/ or *Chrysemys picta*	4 carapace fragments
3	Soft-shelled turtle	*Trionyx* sp.	1 plastron fragment
3	Turkey	*Meleagris gallopavo*	1 humerus fragment
3	Duck	*Anas* spp.	6 fragments of meta-carpi, coracoid
3	Wood duck	*Aix sponsa*	2 humeri sections
3	Unidentified bird bones, probably duck		10 fragments
3	Muskrat	*Ondatra zibethica*	1 pelvis
			1 tibia
			1 ulna
3	Raccoon	*Procyon lotor*	1 ulna
3	Bobcat	*Lynx rufus*	1 dentary fragment
3	Woodchuck	*Marmota monax*	1 lower incisor
3	Catfish	*Ictalurus* spp.	7 spine and jaw fragments
3	Freshwater drum	*Aplodinotus grunniens*	1 pharyngeal bone
3	Bowfin	*Amia calva*	1 skull fragment
3	Unidentified fish bones		20 bones
3	Unidentifiable bone fragments; most large mammal, and probably deer		227 fragments
4	Spike	*Elliptio dilatatus*	25 valves
4	Pink heel-splitter	*Proptera alata*	2 valves
4	Pocketbook	*Lampsilis ventricosa*	1 valve
4	Fat mucket	*Lampsilis siliquoidea*	7 valves
4	Yellow sand-shell or slough sand-shell	*Lampsilis anodontoides* or *L. fallaciosa*	1 valve
4	Mucket	*Actinonaias carinata*	3 valves
4	Pimple-back	*Quadrula pustulosa*	2 valves
4	Buckhorn	*Tritogonia verrucosa*	1 valve
4	Rock pocketbook	*Arcidens confragosus*	1 valve
4	Blue point	*Amblema peruviana*	12 valves
4	Pigtoe	*Fusconaia undata*	1 valve
4	Washboard	*Megalonaias gigantea*	3 valves
4	Niggerhead	*Fusconaia ebenus*	1 valve

Level	Common Name	Species	Specimens
4	Unidentifiable mussel shell fragments		24 valves
4	White-tailed deer	*Odocoileus virginianus*	3 scapulae
			1 humerus
			3 antler fragments
			1 tarsus
			1 calcaneus
			2 radii
			1 carpal
			2 metatarsi
			3 ribs
			9 phalanges
			1 vertebra
			3 ulnae
			4 pelves
			5 dentary
			2 maxillary
			4 teeth
4	Elk	*Cervus canadensis*	1 tarsus
			5 phalanges
4	Beaver	*Castor canadensis*	1 incisor
4	Raccoon	*Procyon lotor*	½ dentary
			1 ulna
4	Striped skunk	*Mephitis mephitis*	1 femur
4	Mink	*Mustela vison*	½ dentary
4	Muskrat	*Ondatra zibethica*	1 femur
4	Duck	*Anas* sp.	1 humerus fragment
4	Turkey	*Meleagris gallopavo*	1 humerus fragment
4	Unidentifiable bird bones		12 fragments
4	Freshwater drum	*Aplodinotus grunniens*	2 pharyngeal bones
			1 otolith
4	Catfish	*Ictalurus* spp.	10 spine and skull fragments
4	Unidentifiable fish bones		34 fragments
4	Pond terrapin and/ or painted turtle	*Pseudemys scripta* and/ or *Chrysemys picta*	13 carapace fragments
4	Unidentifiable bone fragments; most are large mammal and probably deer		366 fragments
5	Washboard	*Megalonaias gigantea*	2 valves
5	Buckhorn	*Tritogonia verrucosa*	1 valve
5	Pink heel-splitter	*Proptera alata*	3 valves
5	Niggerhead	*Fusconaia ebenus*	2 valves
5	Pigtoe	*Fusconaia undata*	3 valves
5	Small niggerhead	*Pleurobema cordatum*	1 valve
5	Floater	*Anodonta* sp. (probably *A. grandis*)	1 valve
5	Pocketbook	*Lampsilis ventricosa*	2 valves
5	Slough sand-shell	*Lampsilis fallaciosa*	4 valves
5	Fat mucket	*Lampsilis siliquoidea*	7 valves
5	Mucket	*Actinonaias carinata*	3 valves
5	Spike	*Elliptio dilatatus*	11 valves

Level	Common Name	Species	Specimens
5	Elephant's ear	*Elliptio crassidens*	1 valve
5	Black sand-shell	*Ligumia recta*	1 valve
5	Blue point	*Amblema peruviana*	21 valves
5	Unidentifiable mussel shell fragments		34 valves
5	White-tailed deer	*Odocoileus virginianus*	2 radii
			2 scapulae
			2 metacarpi
			1 ulna
			5 tibiae
			1 carpal
			1 calcaneus
			1 sternum
			1 rib
			1 vertebra
			1 femur
			1 dentary
			3 teeth
			6 phalanges
			3 tarsi
5	Elk	*Cervus canadensis*	2 phalanges
5	Pond terrapin and/ or painted turtle	*Pseudemys scripta* and/ or *Chrysemys picta*	3 carapace fragments
5	Soft-shelled turtle	*Trionyx* sp.	1 plastron fragment
5	Muskrat	*Ondatra zibethica*	½ dentary
5	Canada goose	*Branta canadensis*	1 humerus section
5	Turkey	*Meleagris gallopavo*	1 humerus
			1 pelvis
			1 femur
5	Unidentifiable bird bones		5 fragments
5	Canid	*Canis* sp.	1 tibia
5	Freshwater drum	*Aplodinotus grunniens*	1 otolith
			1 pharyngeal bone
5	Gar	*Lepisosteus* sp.	2 jaw fragments
5	Catfish	*Ictalurus* spp.	4 spines
			1 skull fragment
5	Bowfin	*Amia calva*	1 skull fragment
5	Unidentifiable fish bones		60 fragments
5	Unidentifiable bone fragments; most are large mammal and probably deer		370
6	Pocket book	*Lampsilis ventricosa*	3 valves
6	Fat mucket	*Lampsilis siliquoidea*	9 valves
6	Slough sand-shell	*Lampsilis fallaciosa*	4 valves
6	Black sand-shell	*Ligumia recta*	1 valve
6	Pigtoe	*Fusconaia undata*	1 valve
6	Niggerhead	*Fusconaia ebenus*	1 valve
6	Pimple-back	*Quadrula pustulosa*	1 valve
6	Purple warty-back	*Cyclonaias tuberculata*	1 valve
6	Pink heel-splitter	*Proptera alata*	3 valves
6	Blue point	*Amblema peruviana*	15 valves
6	Mucket	*Actinonaias carinata*	4 valves

Level	Common Name	Species	Specimens
6	Washboard	*Megalonaias gigantea*	1 valve
6	Spike	*Elliptio dilatatus*	17 valves
6	Elephant's ear	*Elliptio crassidens*	3 valves
6	Unidentifiable mussel shell fragments		21 valves
6	White-tailed deer	*Odocoileus virginianus*	2 antler fragments
			2 vertebrae
			2 scapulae
			4 ulnae
			2 calcaneae
			3 pelves fragments
			1 maxillary
			1 dentary
			2 teeth
			3 phalanges
			3 humeri
			3 radii
			3 tibiae
			4 tarsi
			2 metatarsi
			2 metacarpi
6	Elk	*Cervus canadensis*	1 tooth
			1 tarsus
			1 phalange
6	Pond terrapin and/ or painted turtle	*Pseudemys scripta* and/ or *Chrysemys picta*	26 carapace fragments
6	Turkey	*Meleagris gallopavo*	1 tarsometatarsus
			1 coracoid
6	Unidentifiable bird bones		8 fragments
6	Striped skunk	*Mephitis mephitis*	1 radius
6	Freshwater drum	*Aplodinotus grunniens*	1 pharyngeal bone
6	River redhorse	*Moxostoma carinatum*	1 pharyngeal bone and teeth
6	Catfish	*Ictalurus* spp.	5 spine and skull fragments
6	Bowfin	*Amia calva*	1 skull fragment
6	Unidentifiable fish bones		23 fragments
6	Unidentifiable bone fragments; most are large mammal and probably deer		308 fragments

APPENDIX B

SUMMARY OF FAUNA FROM TEST PIT I

Identifier: Paul W. Parmalee, Curator of Zoology,
Illinois State Museum, Springfield

Common Name	Species	Number of Specimens
Spike	*Elliptio dilatatus*	83
Blue point	*Amblema peruviana*	67
Fat mucket	*Lampsilis siliquoidea*	30
Mucket	*Actinonaias carinata*	16
Slough sand-shell	*Lampsilis fallaciosa*	10
Pink heel-splitter	*Proptera alata*	10
Washboard	*Megalonaias gigantea*	8
Pocketbook	*Lampsilis ventricosa*	7
Pigtoe	*Fusconaia undata*	6
Niggerhead	*Fusconaia ebenus*	5
Pimple-back	*Quadrula pustulosa*	4
Elephant's ear	*Elliptio crassidens*	4
Small niggerhead	*Pleurobema cordatum*	2
Buckhorn	*Tritogonia verrucosa*	2
Black sand-shell	*Ligumia recta*	2
Yellow sand-shell	*Lampsilis anodontoides*	1
Butterfly	*Plagiola lineolata*	1
Rock pocketbook	*Arcidens confragosus*	1
Floater	*Anodonta* sp.	1
Purple warty-back	*Cyclonaias tuberculata*	1
Unidentifiable mussel shell fragments		133
Catfish	*Ictalurus* spp.	23
Freshwater drum	*Aplodinotus grunniens*	10
Bowfin	*Amia calva*	3
Gar	*Lepisosteus* sp.	2
River redhorse	*Moxostoma carinatum*	1
Unidentifiable fish bones		141
Pond terrapin, Painted turtle, and/or Map turtles	*Pseudemys scripta*, *Chrysemys picta*, and/or *Graptemys* spp.	47
Soft-shelled turtle	*Trionyx* sp.	2
Pond terrapin	*Pseudemys scripta*	1
White-tailed deer	*Odocoileus virginianus*	145
Elk	*Cervus canadensis*	12
Muskrat	*Ondatra zibethica*	5
Raccoon	*Procyon lotor*	3
Striped skunk	*Mephitis mephitis*	2
Canid	*Canis* sp.	2
Bobcat	*Lynx rufus*	1
Woodchuck	*Marmota monax*	1
Beaver	*Castor canadensis*	1
Mink	*Mustela vison*	1

Common Name	Species	Number of Specimens
Unidentifiable fragments; most are large mammal and probably deer		1,387
Duck	*Anas* spp.	9
Turkey	*Meleagris gallopavo*	7
Canada goose	*Branta canadensis*	1
Unidentifiable bird bones		37

APPENDIX C

FAUNA FROM TEST PITS II AND III AND THEIR EXTENSIONS

Identifier: Paul W. Parmalee, Curator of Zoology,
Illinois State Museum, Springfield

Common Name	Species	Number of Specimens
Freshwater drum	*Aplodinotus grunniens*	32
Channel catfish and/or Blue catfish	*Ictalurus lacustris* and/or *I. furcatus*	18
Buffalo fish and suckers	*Catostomidae*	14
Bullhead	*Ictalurus* sp.	12
Gar	*Lepisosteus* sp.	12
Catfish	*Ictalurus* sp.	10
Bowfin	*Amia calva*	9
Bigmouth buffalo fish	*Ictiobus cyprinellus*	4
Redhorse sucker	*Moxostomy* sp.	3
Bass	*Micropterus* sp.	3
Flathead catfish	*Pylodictis olivaris*	1
Longnose gar	*Lepisosteus osseus*	1
Smallmouth buffalo fish or Black buffalo fish	*Ictiobus bubalus* or *I. niger*	1
Pike	*Esox* sp., probably *E. lucius*	1
Painted turtle, Map turtles, and/or Pond terrapin; most are probably pond terrapin	*Chrysemys picta*, *Graptemys* spp., and/or *Pseudemys scripta;* most are probably *Pseudemys*	65
Soft-shelled turtle	*Trionyx* sp.	6
Pond terrapin	*Pseudemys scripta*	5
Snapping turtle	*Chelydra serpentina*	5
Turkey	*Meleagris gallopavo*	26
Canada goose	*Branta canadensis*	13
Trumpeter swan	*Olor buccinator*	4
Wood duck	*Aix sponsa*	2
Ring-necked duck or Lesser scaup	*Aythya collaris* or *A. affinis*	1
Blue-winged teal	*Anas discors*	1
Red-tailed hawk	*Buted jamaicensis*	1
Redhead	*Aythya americana*	1
Gadwall	*Anas strepera*	1
American bittern	*Botaurus lentiginosus*	1
Marbled godwit	*Limosa fedoa*	1
Mallard	*Anas platyrhynchos*	1
American coot	*Fulica americana*	1
Pied-billed grebe	*Podilymbus podiceps*	3
White-tailed deer	*Odocoileus virginianus*	366
Elk	*Cervus canadensis*	63
Beaver	*Castor canadensis*	22
Raccoon	*Procyon lotor*	12
Muskrat	*Ondatra zibethica*	5

Common Name	Species	Number of Specimens
Man	*Homo sapiens*	5
Striped skunk	*Mephitis mephitis*	3
Woodchuck	*Marmota monax*	3
Canid	*Canis* sp., possibly dog *C. familiaris*	3
Otter	*Lutra canadensis*	1
Red fox	*Vulpes fulva*	1
Bog lemming	*Synaptomys cooperi*	1
Unidentifiable large mammal fragments, most probably deer and elk		2,678
Unidentifiable fish bone fragments		96
Unidentifiable bird bone fragments		70

APPENDIX D

OTHER FAUNA FROM THE STEUBEN VILLAGE SITE

Identifiers, University of Michigan: Dr. Reeve Bailey, Fish; Dr. Norman Hartweg, Turtle; Dr. Emmet Hooper, Mammals; Dr. Philip Humphrey, Birds; Dr. Henry van der Schalie, Shell

Common Name	Species	Specimen
Pocketbook	*Lampsilis ventricosa*	3 valves
Mucket	*Actinonaias carinata*	1 valve
Washboard	*Megalonaias gigantea*	2 valves
Pink heel-splitter	*Proptera alata*	2 valves
Blue point	*Amblema peruviana*	3 valves
Freshwater drum	*Aplodinotus grunniens*	several bones
Gar	*Lepisosteus* sp. (Probably *platostomus*)	several bones
Pond terrapin	*Pseudemys scripta*	5 shell and bone fragments
Soft-shelled turtle	*Trionyx* sp.	2 shell and bone fragments
White-tailed deer	*Odocoileus virginianus*	7 sacrums
		6 pelves
		34 broken long bones
		6 phalanges
		3 skull fragments
		6 mandible fragments
		6 ribs
		5 vertebrae
		11 unworked antler fragments
Elk	*Cervus canadensis*	2 broken long bones
		2 broken mandibles
		- several loose teeth
		2 phalanges
		1 antler fragment
Dog	*Canis familiaris*	1 nearly complete specimen
Black bear	*Ursus americanus*	1 canine
Beaver	*Castor canadensis*	1 broken mandible
Woodchuck	*Marmota monax*	3 mandibles
		8 long bones
Trumpeter swan	*Olor buccinator*	1 humerus
		1 radius
Swan	*Olor* sp.	1 ulna
Turkey	*Meleagris gallopavo*	2 humeri
Canada goose	*Branta canadensis*	1 humerus
Unidentifiable bird bones		2 fragmentary long bones

APPENDIX E

FAUNA FROM THE STEUBEN MOUNDS

Identifiers, University of Michigan: Dr. Emmet Hooper, Mammals; Dr. Philip Humphrey, Birds; Dr. Henry van der Schalie, Shell

Common Name	Species	Specimen	Locus
Raccoon	*Procyon lotor*	Skull	Burial 27, Mound 1
		Broken mandible	Burials 1 and 2, Mound 3
Cottontail	*Sylvilagus floridanus*	Complete specimen	In fill over Pit B, Mound 1
Woodchuck	*Marmota monax*	Several complete and partial specimens	Throughout fill of Mound 1
Dog	*Canis familiaris*	Complete specimen	Near Pit A, Mound 1
Turkey	*Meleagris*	Complete leg	Between Pits B and C, Mound 1
Conch shell	*Busycon perversum*	Altered into a vessel	Burial 41, Mound 1

APPENDIX F

SKULLDUGGERY: A DAY AMONG DEAD MEN'S BONES

Peoria Daily Transcript, September 28, 1877

The morning train yesterday on the C.R.I. & P. Railway went northward with a small party of members of the Peoria Scientific Association and their friends bound upon an exploring expedition among the monuments of the past, in other words, to open a mound, "and unearth whatever might be found therein." It is well known that in the lower part of Marshall County on both sides of the River these mounds are very numerous being built apparently according to their location and shape for three purposes: of defense, of worship, and of sepulture. Of these the most interesting to the antiquary and the ethnologist are those used as burial places and upon one of these the Peoria searchers were so fortunate as to fall yesterday. The party consisted of Drs. Chapman, Brendall, and Breed, Mr. and Mrs. B. L. T. Bourland, Mrs. Emma Smith, Mrs. Rogers, Mr. W. F. Bryan, Rev. Mr. Gardner, Mr. John Chalmers, and the Transcript's representative. The expedition was undertaken in company with a party from Lacon and vicinity. The mound which it was decided to explore was situated a short distance this side of Sparland and the gentlemanly conductor very kindly showed up and dropped off the Peorians directly opposite their objective point. Climbing the fence and making their way a short distance to the field, evidence of occupation was seen in several wagons with their attendant horses who were quietly stabled under the trees. The owners of these teams were the forerunners of the Laconites who by twos and threes dropped in until the following ladies and gentlemen were present: G. F. Whiteman and wife, Spencer Ellsworth, Robert O'Hara, Dr. Tessmer, Mrs. Meiner, Mr. and Mrs. Silas Hutchens, Rev. Mr. Tracy, Mr. Gage, Mr. and Mrs. Titus, J. R. Chapman and daughter, and Mr. L. M. Culver. There also was present Mr. William Gifford of Alta and his son and daughter. Col. Fort looked in for a few minutes about lunch time and there must have been others whom we failed to note. A little time was spent in preliminary examination and observation and finally about half past eleven active operations were begun. Captain Whiteman, who was the leading spirit in the operations of the day, had engaged the services of a quartette of stout laborers and they were set to work to dig a hole in the top of one of the best defined and apparently the most promising of the many mounds with which the brow of the bluff was dotted. Under their vigorous efforts the top of the mound was quickly removed and the anxious scientists and non-scientists looked on waiting eagerly to see what they might see as the work of excavation went on. Presently a cry of delight was heard "there's something," and at once the practical vulgar work of digging with pick and spade was suspended and several of the more enthusiastic collectors including one lady who objects to having her name mentioned clambored into the hole and began working with knives and fingers. The "thing" proved to be a human skull in a most excellent state of preservation. It was taken out almost whole. When it was finally disentombed and held up to view there was a simultaneous rush among the whole company to see which should say "Alas poor Yorick!"

While this work was going on a number of the ladies had disappeared and about this time a number of "hellos" indicated that something was going on in the valley below. The "thing" had proved to be luncheon which was provided by the Lacon section of the party and to which ample justice was done by all. The coffee was excellent and the sandwiches were good. The cake was rich and the fruit was ripe, the welcome was hardy, the appetite was prodigious. What more could be asked for a dinner party in the woods or out of them.

Dinner over the party returned to the mound and until train time were busily engaged in excavation. Three more skulls and a large number of human bones all in a fair state of preservation were taken out. Also the most important find of the day, an earthen bowl almost perfect. This was taken possession of by the Secretary of the Scientific Association who would hardly allow it to go out of her hands and who, when we saw her last, was still clinging to it in a way which indicated that she believed it would be worth at least three grasshoppers and a beetle. At about four o'clock the whistle of the returning train was heard and all hands of the Peorian's hastened to the track. The train stopped and took us on and in a brief time we were home again.

If we had been a scientific individual we should have talked earnestly in this account of craniums and occiputs, of femurs and tibia, of osteology and numerous other ologies. But had we attempted we should only have displayed our ignorance without adding anything to the stock of knowledge of our readers. Therefore and above all of which we saw a part of which we were we had given only a running sketch of an exposition which will long be marked with a white stone of memory of these who participated in it. If any of the scientists want to write a scientific account of the finds the columns of the Transcript shall be opened to them.

APPENDIX G

THE MOUND BUILDERS

Peoria Daily Transcript, September 29, 1877

We gave yesterday an account of the opening of the mound near Sparland on the previous day. All through the upper end at least of the Illinois valley these mounds are very numerous. Captain Whiteman of Lacon had located a map within a comparatively short area near the Black Patridge Creek near Woodford County. Thirty-six mounds are clearly and distinctly marked and on the west side of the river there is also a very large number. In a field on the lower side of the railway a short distance above Chillicothe is one of the largest and best preserved mounds known. That these were made by the Indian inhabitants of the county there is no doubt and it is probable that a considerable part of them at least are burial places. Apparently very little has been done in exploring any of them though they are almost sure to return rich rewards to the searchers. Later the attention of the Peoria Scientific Association has been attracted toward them and an effort will be made to have a thorough scientific examination on one or more of these mounds this fall. The party whose adventures we sketched yesterday was but the forerunner of more important work. We trust the Society will not let the matter drop. Peoria and vicinity as is well known has many large Indian villages and it is probable that much white fighting was done here. In these mounds are very likely to be found pottery implements of value illustrating the former history of the region. The finds in one mound may not unlikely prove of more value than all the cost of securing them.

APPENDIX H

MORE MOUND DIGGING

Peoria Daily Transcript, October 8, 1877

Miss Emma Smith, the Assistant State Entomologist furnished the following particulars of another mound exploring expedition. A party from Peoria consisting of Messrs. Bourland, Bryan, White, Cochran, and others in conjunction with quite a large party from Lacon including Col. Fort and wife, Captain Wightman and wife, D. B. Weir, and others last Saturday proceeded to the mound where they commenced operations one week ago near Sparland and found more remains of both children and grown people. Also two teeth belonging to a bear. These teeth were pierced with holes and had evidently been worn as ornaments. One of them was in an excellent state of preservation. The party opened four other mounds but found only charred bones. They contemplated going to Mossville next week and will open a number of mounds two miles beyond that place.

LITERATURE CITED

Baker, Frank C., James B. Griffin, Richard G. Morgan, Georg K. Neumann, and Jay L. B. Taylor

1941 Contributions to the Archaeology of the Illinois River Valley. Transactions of the American Philosophical Society, N.S., 32, Pt. 1. Philadelphia.

Barrett, Samuel A.

1933 Ancient Aztalan. Bulletin of the Public Museum of the City of Milwaukee, 13. Milwaukee, Wis.

Bennett, John W.

1945 Archaeological Explorations in Jo Daviess County, Illinois. Chicago: The University of Chicago Press.

Cameron, Peter

1953 Comparison of the Artifact Assemblages from two Hopewell Sites. Journal of Illinois State Archaeological Society, N.S., 3, No. 3:75-77.

Cole, Fay-Cooper, and Thorne Deuel

1937 Rediscovering Illinois: Archaeological Explorations in and around Fulton County. Chicago: The University of Chicago Press.

Cole, Fay-Cooper, and others

1951 Kincaid: A Prehistoric Illinois Metropolis. Chicago: The University of Chicago Press.

Cooper, L. R.

1933 Red Cedar Variant of the Wisconsin Hopewell. Bulletin of the Public Museum of the City of Milwaukee, 16, No. 2. Milwaukee.

Culin, Stewart

1907 Games of the North American Indians. Twenty-fourth Annual Report of the Bureau of American Ethnology, 1902-1903, pp. 1-846. Washington, D.C.

Deuel, Thorne

1952 Hopewellian Dress in Illinois. *In:* Archaeology of the Eastern United States, James B. Griffin, ed. Chicago: The University of Chicago Press, pp. 165-75.

Flecker, H.

1954 Time of Appearance and Fusion of Ossification Centers as Observed by Roentgenographic Methods. *In:* Basic Readings on the Identification of Human Skeletons: Estimation of Age, T. Dale Stewart and Mildred Trotter, eds. Wenner-Gren Foundation for Anthropological Research, Inc., pp. 97-159. New York.

Fowler, Melvin L.
1952 The Clear Lake Site: Hopewellian Occupation. *In:* Hopewellian Communities in Illinois, Thorne Deuel, ed. Scientific Papers, Illinois State Museum, 5, No. 4:131-74. Springfield.

Griffin, James B.
1941 Additional Hopewell Material from Illinois. Indiana Historical Society, Prehistory Research Series, 2, No. 3. Indianapolis.
1943 The Fort Ancient Aspect, Its Cultural and Chronological Position in Mississippi Valley Archaeology. Ann Arbor: The University of Michigan Press.
1946 Cultural Change and Continuity in Eastern United States Archaeology. *In:* Man in Northeastern North America, Frederick Johnson, ed. Papers of the Robert S. Peabody Foundation for Archaeology, 3:37-95. Andover, Mass.
1952 Some Early and Middle Woodland Pottery Types in Illinois. *In:* Hopewellian Communities in Illinois, Thorne Deuel, ed. Scientific Papers, Illinois State Museum, 5, No. 3:93-129. Springfield.
1955 Observations on the Grooved Axe in North America. Pennsylvania Archaeologist Bulletin, 25, No. 1:31-43.
1958 The Chronological Position of the Hopewellian Culture in the Eastern United States. Anthropological Papers, Museum of Anthropology, The University of Michigan, No. 12. Ann Arbor.

Guthe, Carl E. (Chairman)
1937 The Indianapolis Archaeological Conference. Committee on State Archaeological Surveys, Division of Anthropology and Psychology, National Research Council. Washington, D.C. (Mimeographed.)

Kellar, James H.
1955 The Atlatl in North America. Indiana Historical Society Prehistory Research Series, 3, No. 3. Indianapolis.

Kidder, Alfred V.
1932 The Artifacts of Pecos. Phillips Academy, Department of Archaeology. Andover, Mass.

Kroeber, Alfred L.
1948 Anthropology. New York: Harcourt, Brace & Company.

Lewis, T. M. N., and Madeline Kneberg, Eds.
1956 Ten Years of the Tennessee Archaeologist. Chattanooga: J. B. Graham.

McGregor, John C.
1952 The Havana Site. *In:* Hopewellian Communities in Illinois, Thorne Deuel, ed. Scientific Papers, Illinois State Museum, 5, No. 2:43-91. Springfield.
1958 The Pool and Irving Villages: A Study of Hopewell Occupation in the Illinois River Valley. Urbana: University of Illinois Press.

McKern, W. C.
1931 A Wisconsin Variant of the Hopewell Culture. Bulletin of the Public Museum of the City of Milwaukee, 10, No. 2. Milwaukee.

McKern, W. C., P. F. Titterington, and James B. Griffin
1945 Painted Pottery Figurines from Illinois. American Antiquity, 10, No. 3:295-302.

Mills, William C.
1906 Baum Prehistoric Village. Ohio Archaeological and Historical Quarterly, 15, No. 1:44-136. Columbus.
1909 Explorations of the Seip Mound. *In:* Certain Mounds and Village Sites in Ohio, 2, Pt. 1 (1917):1-100. Columbus.
1922 Explorations of the Feurt Mounds and Village Site. *In:* Certain Mounds and Village Sites in Ohio, 3, No. 1:1-149. Columbus.

Mohrman, Robert, and Harold Mohrman
1950 The Rock Creek Site in Adams County, Illinois. Journal of Illinois State Archaeological Society, N.S., 1, No. 2:57-59.

Moore, Clarence B.
1916 Some Aboriginal Sites on Green River, Kentucky. Journal of the Academy of Natural Sciences of Philadelphia, 16:440-87. Philadelphia.

Moorehead, Warren K., and others
1928 The Cahokia Mounds. University of Illinois Bulletin, 26, No. 4. Urbana.

Moroney, M. J.
1957 Facts from Figures. Pelican Books, A-236. Baltimore.

Morse, Dan, George Schoenbeck, and Dan F. Morse
1953 Fiedler Site. Journal of Illinois State Archaeological Society, 3, No. 2:34-46.

Morse, Dan F.
1956 Some of the Sexual Characteristics Found in Human Bones. Central States Archaeological Journal, 2, No. 3:94-96.
1957 The Estimation of Age of Skeletal Material. Central States Archaeological Journal, 3, No. 3:89-96.
1959 Preliminary Report on a Red Ocher Mound at the Morse Site, Fulton County, Illinois. Papers of the Michigan Academy of Science, Arts, and Letters, 44:193-207. Ann Arbor: The University of Michigan Press.
1960 The Southern Cult, the Crable Site, Fulton County, Illinois. Central States Archaeological Journal, 7, No. 4:124-35.

Morse, Dan F., and Don F. Dickson
1956 Prehistoric Pathology. Central States Archaeological Journal, 2, No. 4:143-50.

Neumann, Georg K., and Melvin L. Fowler
1952 Hopewellian Sites in the Lower Wabash Valley. *In:* Hopewellian Communities in Illinois, Thorne Deuel, ed. Scientific Papers, Illinois State Museum, 5, No. 5:175-248. Springfield.

Perino, Gregory
1960 The Micro-Drill Industry at Cahokia. Central States Archaeological Journal, 7, No. 3:116-20.

Powell, B. Bruce
1957 Hopewellian Pottery of the Lower Illinois Valley: the Snyders Site Ceramics. Papers of the Michigan Academy of Science, Arts, and Letters, 42:219-24. Ann Arbor: The University of Michigan Press.

Quimby, George I., Jr.
1941 The Goodall Focus: An Analysis of Ten Hopewellian Components in Michigan and Indiana. Indiana Historical Society, Prehistory Research Series, 2, No. 2. Indianapolis.

Schoenbeck, Ethel
1947 A Seven-Pound Copper Axe Among 1946 Hopewell Discoveries. Transactions of the Illinois Academy of Science, 40:36-42.
1948 Steuben Village Site, a Hopewell Village of Central Illinois. *Ibid.*, 41: 19-20.
1949 More Data on Hopewell Sites in Peoria Regions. *Ibid.*, 42:41-46.

Schultz, Floyd, and Albert C. Spaulding
1948 A Hopewellian Burial Site in the Lower Republican Valley, Kansas. American Antiquity, 13, No. 4, Pt. 1:306-13.

Spooner, Harry L.
1940 Old Peoria Newspapers Replete with References to Indians of Vicinity. Quarterly Bulletin of the Illinois State Archaeological Society, 3, No. 1:8-9.

Thomas, Cyrus
1894 Report on the Mound Explorations of the Bureau of Ethnology. Twelfth Annual Report of the Bureau of American Ethnology, 1890-1891, pp. 3-730. Washington, D.C.

Trotter, Mildred, and Goldine Gleser
1952 Estimation of Stature from Longbones of American Whites and Negroes. American Journal of Physical Anthropology, 10, No. 4:463-514.

Walker, Winslow M.
1952 The Dickison Mound Group, Peoria County, Illinois. *In:* Hopewellian Communities in Illinois, Thorne Deuel, ed. Scientific Papers, Illinois State Museum, 5, No. 1:12-41. Springfield.

Webb, William S.
1946 Indian Knoll. The University of Kentucky Reports in Anthropology and Archaeology, 4, No. 3, Pt. 1. Lexington.
1950 The Read Shell Midden Site, Site 10, Butler County, Kentucky. The University of Kentucky Reports in Anthropology, 7, No. 5. Lexington.

Webb, William S., and David L. De Jarnette
1942 An Archaeological Survey of Pickwick Basin in the Adjacent Portions of the States of Alabama, Mississippi and Tennessee. Bureau of American Ethnology, Bull. 129. Washington, D.C.

Webb, William S., and William G. Haag
1940 Cypress Creek Village Sites 11 and 12, McLean County, Kentucky. The University of Kentucky Reports in Anthropology, 4, No. 2. Lexington.

Wedel, Waldo A.
1943 Archaeological Investigations in Platte and Clay Counties, Missouri. United States National Museum, Bull. 183. Washington, D.C.

Wilford, Lloyd A.
1955 A Revised Classification of the Prehistoric Cultures of Minnesota. American Antiquity, 21, No. 2:130-42.

Willoughby, Charles C.
1935 Antiquities of the New England Indians. Cambridge, Mass.

Winters, Eric, Jr., R. S. Smith, and L. H. Smith
1937 Marshall County Soils. University of Illinois Agricultural Experiment Station, Soil Report No. 59. Urbana.

Wray, Charles F., and Harry L. Schoff
1953 A Preliminary Report on the Seneca Sequence in Western New York, 1550-1687. Pennsylvania Archaeologist, 23, No. 2:53-63.

PLATES

PLATE I

Fig. 1. Test Pit I, Steuben site. Dr. Dan Morse is standing in the excavation. View toward the northwest.

Fig. 2. Test Pit II and extension. View toward northwest.

PLATE II

Fig. 1. Test Pit III extension. View to north. Plow-torn burial.

Fig. 2. Hummel Dentate Stamped (upper right and lower left) and Naples Dentate Stamped, Steuben site. UMMA Neg. 11026.

PLATE III

Fig. 1. Steuben Punctated, Steuben site. UMMA Neg. 11025.

Fig. 2. Steuben Punctated, Steuben site. Lower right two sherds are similar to Weaver in paste. UMMA Neg. 11029.

PLATE IV

Fig. 1. Weaver sherds, Steuben site. Upper row: Plain Stamped, Plain, and Wavy or Notched Rim. Lower row: chunk of grit-tempered pottery, Cordmarked (with exteriorly protruding nodes), and Plain. UMMA Neg. 11028.

Fig. 2. Upper row from left to right: Baehr Brushed, Hopewell Plain Rocked Stamped (Brangenberg Rim), Hopewell Rim, Havana Miscellaneous Incised, Hopewell Zoned Incised. Middle row: Hopewell Zoned Dentate Rocked Stamped, Hopewell Plain, Naples Barred Ovoid Stamped. Bottom row: Hopewell Plain Rocked Stamped, Hopewell Dentate Rocked Stamped, Neteler Dentate Crescent Stamped, Weaver Incised. Steuben site. UMMA Neg. 11030.

PLATE V

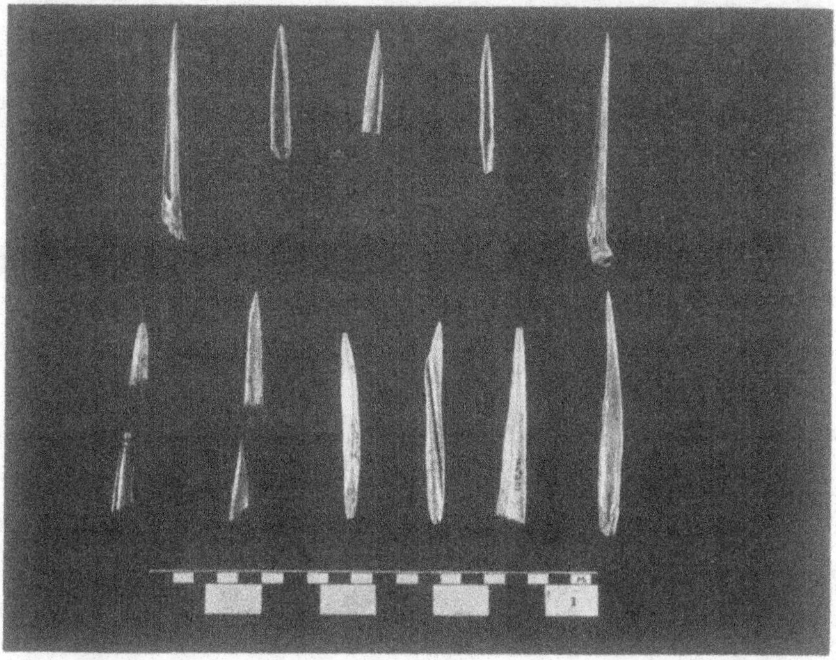

Fig. 1. Bone awls, Steuben site. Top row is split turkey tarso-metatarsus Hopewell type. UMMA Neg. 11014.

Fig. 2. Bone punctator and Steuben Punctated sherd, Steuben site.

PLATE VI

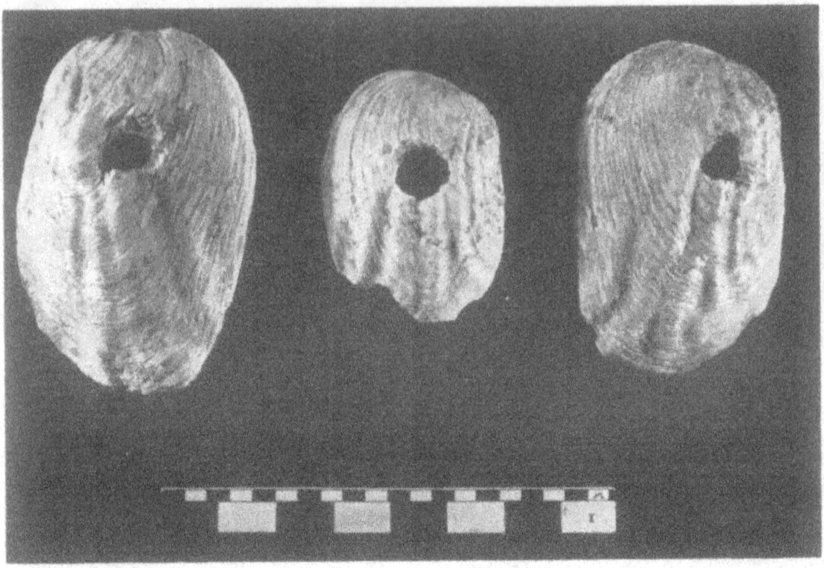

Fig. 1. Shell hoes, Steuben site. UMMA Neg. 11013.

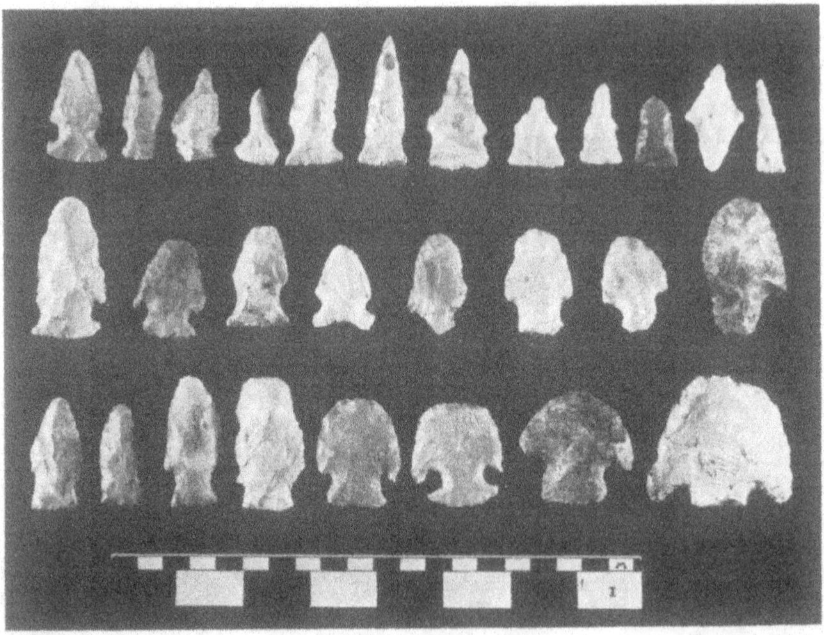

Fig. 2. Drills and notched scrapers and knives, Steuben site. UMMA Neg. 11016.

PLATE VII

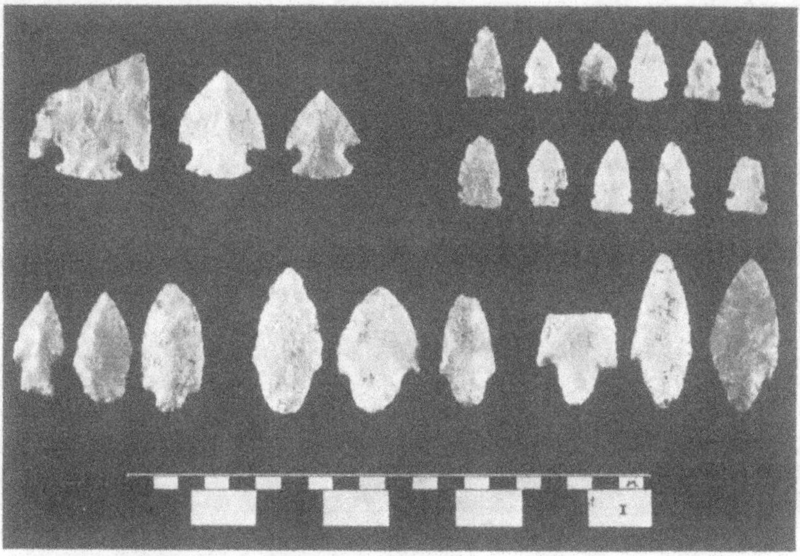

Fig. 1. Steuben site projectile points. Upper left: Snyders Corner Notched. Upper right: Small Triangular. Lower row from left to right: Contracting and straight stemmed, variety straight base, rounded base, and pointed base. UMMA Neg. 11015.

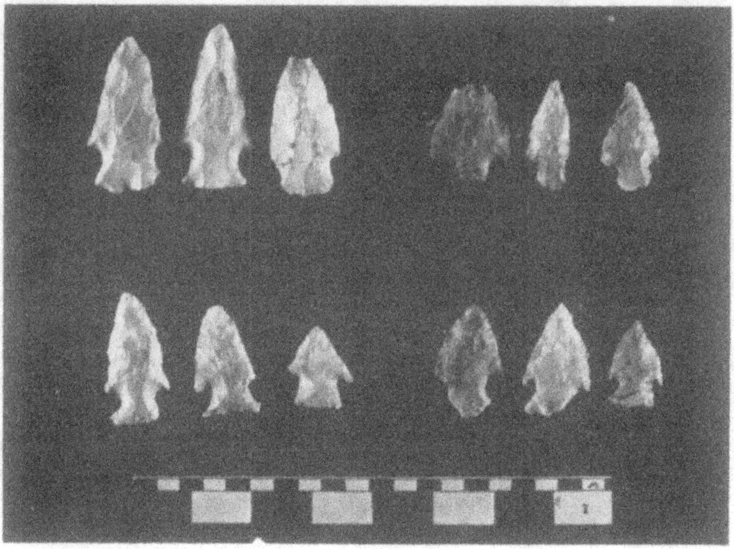

Fig. 2. Marshall Barbed: upper left, variety rugged; upper right, variety crude; lower row, variety fine. Steuben site. UMMA Neg. 11012.

PLATE VIII

Fig. 1. Steuben Expanded Stemmed: top row, variety small and thin; lower left, variety squat and thick; lower right, variety long and slender. Steuben site. UMMA Neg. 11007.

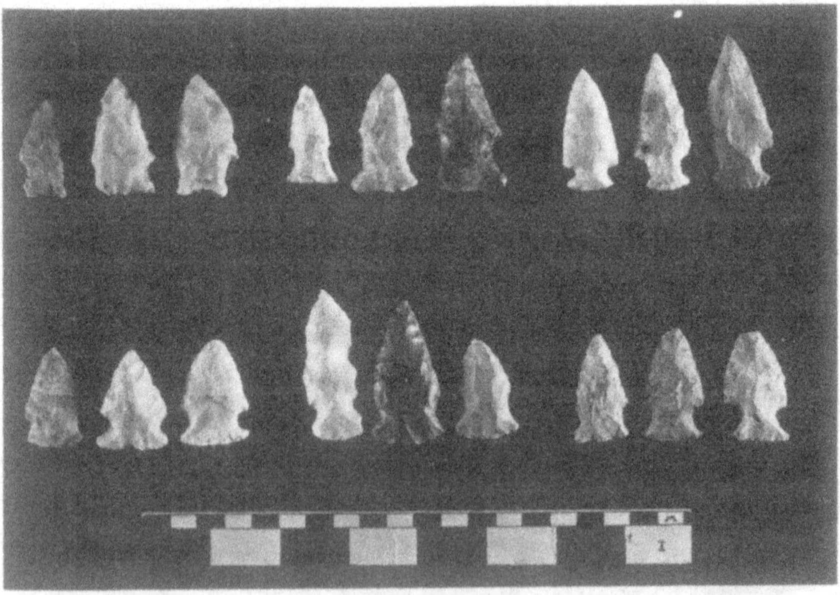

Fig. 2. Large Side Notched, Steuben site. Upper left two and lower left group: variety straight and concave base. Rest: variety convex base. UMMA Neg. 11006.

PLATE IX

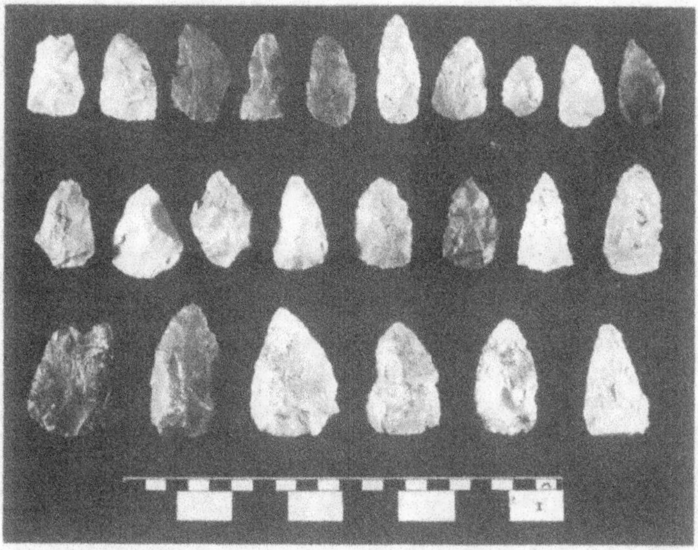

Fig. 1. Triangular Knives, Steuben site. UMMA Neg. 11008.

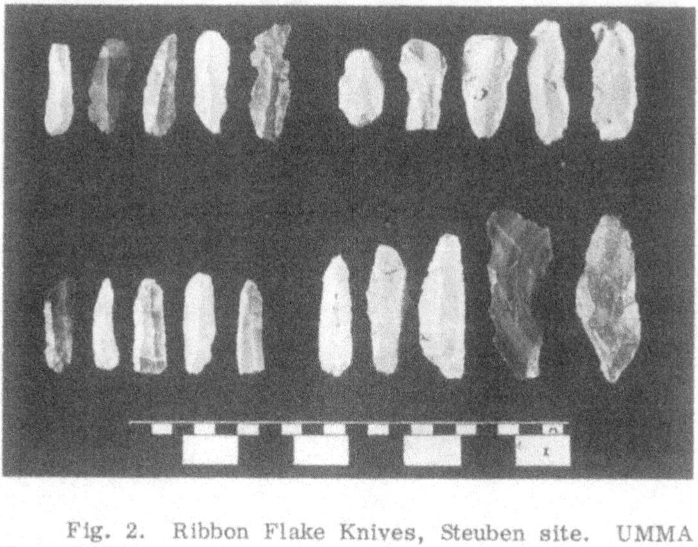

Fig. 2. Ribbon Flake Knives, Steuben site. UMMA Neg. 11005.

PLATE X

Fig. 1. Flint scrapers, Steuben site. UMMA Neg. 11004.

Fig. 2. Hammerstones and stone celts, Steuben site.

PLATE XI

Fig. 1. Stone gorget fragments, Steuben site.

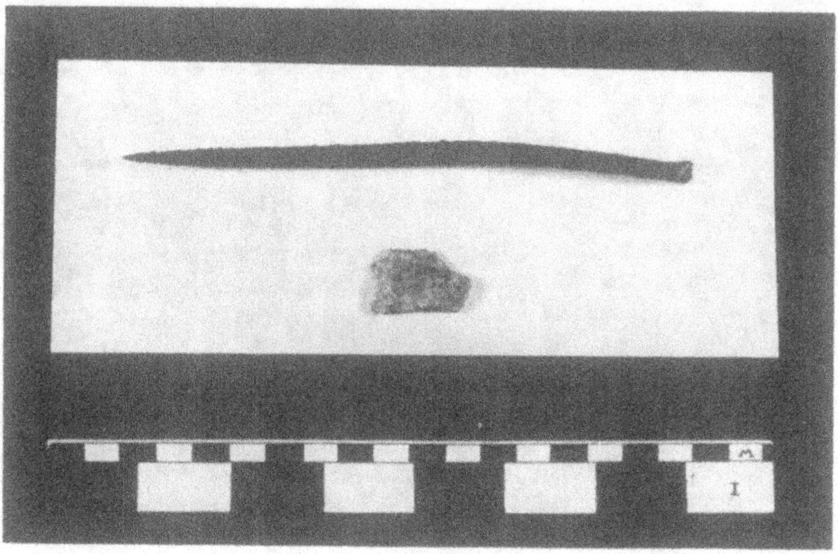

Fig. 2. Copper artifacts, Steuben site. UMMA Neg. 11011.

PLATE XII

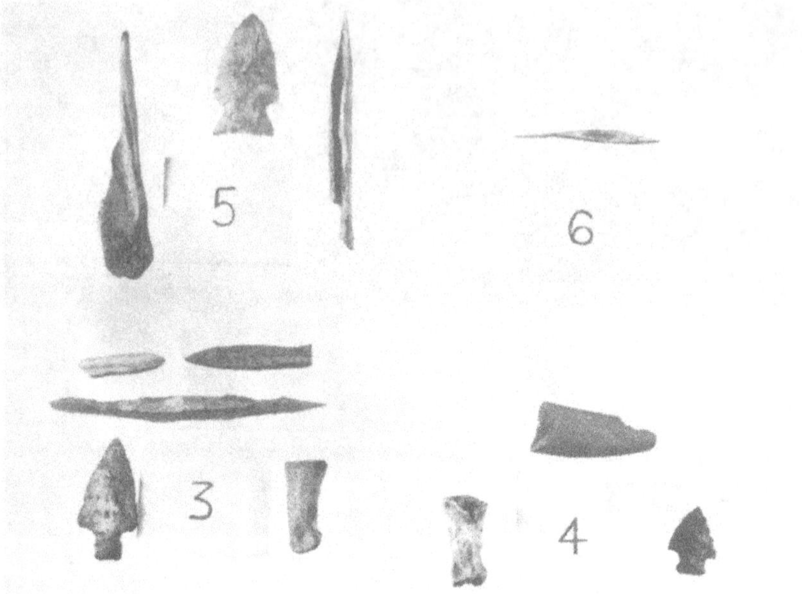

Fig. 1. Artifacts from Test Pit I, Steuben site, by level. UMMA Neg. 11024.

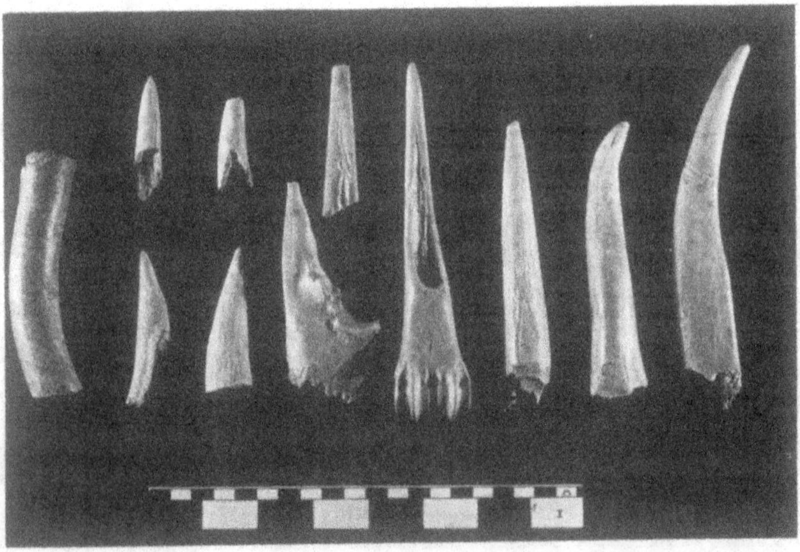

Fig. 2. Bone tools, Steuben site. UMMA Neg. 11009.

PLATE XIII

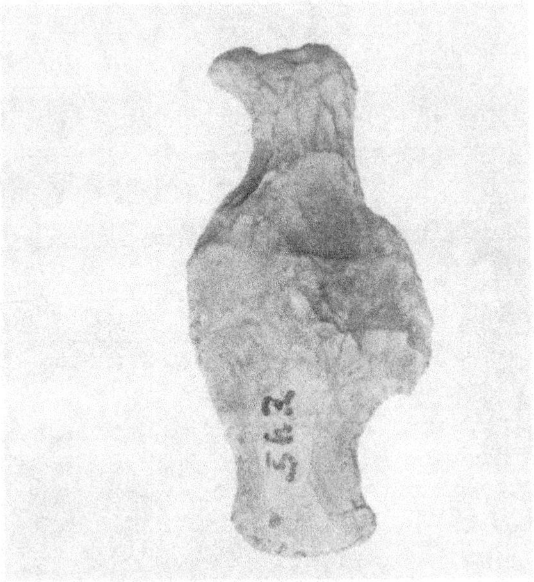

Fig. 1. Flint effigy in the Elliot collection, Steuben site. Length 1-3/4 inches.

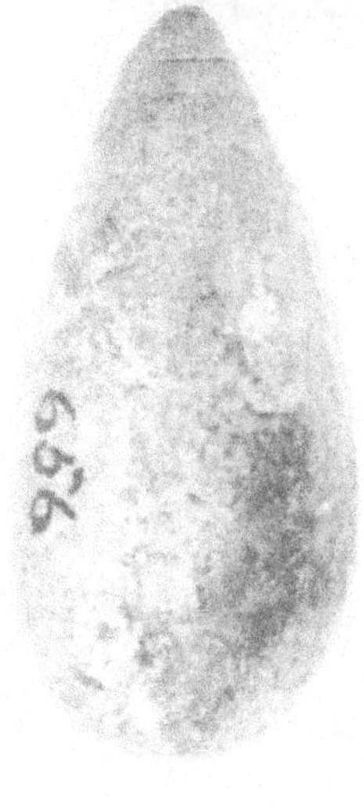

Fig. 2. Stone plummet in the Elliot collection, Steuben site. Length 1-5/8 inches.

Fig. 3. Stone discoidal in the Elliot collection, Steuben site. Diameter 2-1/2 inches.

PLATE XIV

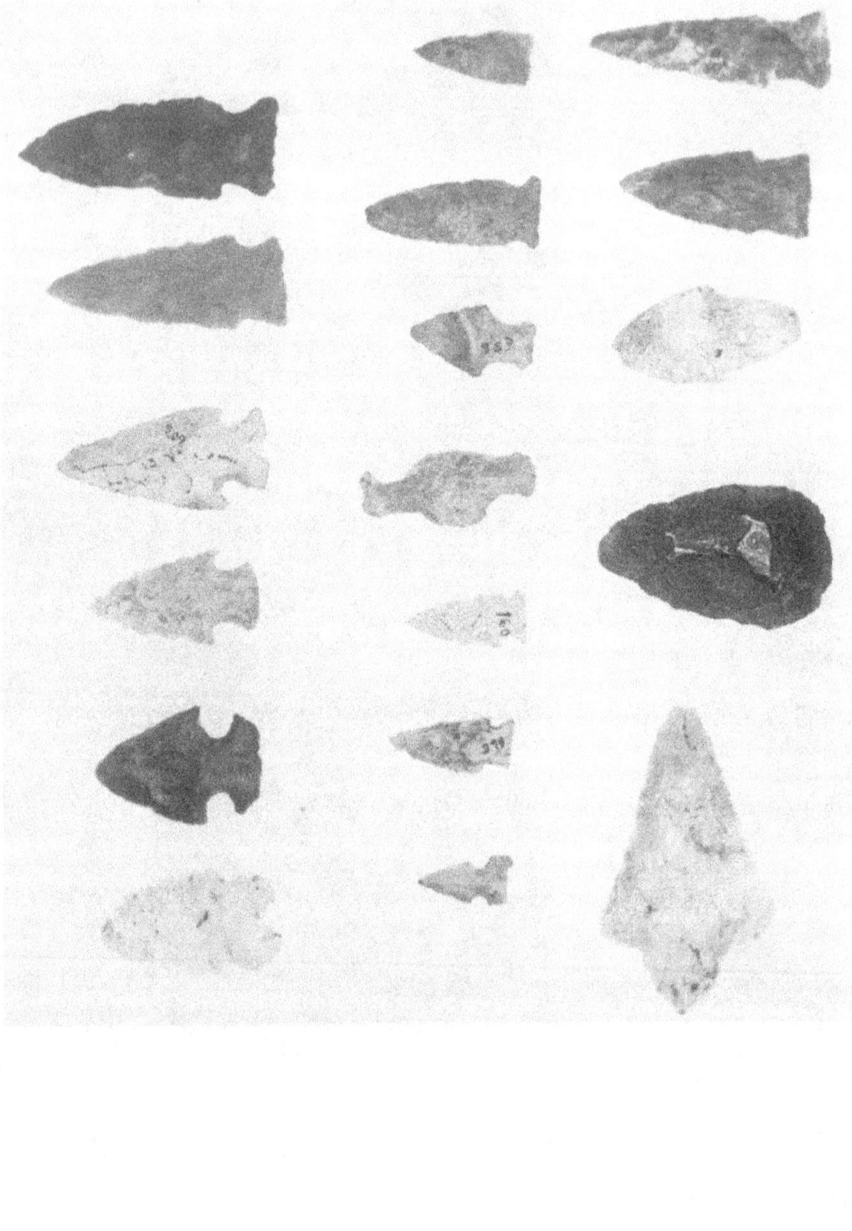

Fig. 1. Artifacts from the Elliot collection, Steuben site. In the center of the lower row is a chipped hematite artifact. Flint effigy in center of middle row is 1-3/4 inches long.

PLATE XV

Fig. 1. View toward southeast from Mound 1. Steuben village site is in cultivated field at lower left-hand corner.

Fig. 2. Mound 1, Steuben site. View toward northeast.

PLATE XVI

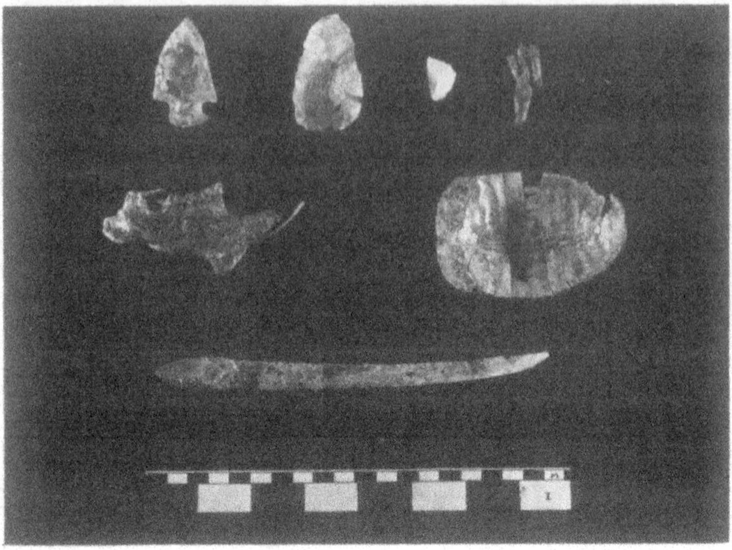

Fig. 1. Top row: Snyders Corner Notched knife from fill of Pit C, Mound 1; Triangular knife and scraper from Mound 1 fill; and scrap of copper from Pit B, Mound 1. Middle row: Beaver jaw associated with disturbed burials in Mound 3; and turtle shell spoon found in vessel associated with Burials 39-41, Mound 1. Bottom: mammal bone spatula associated with Burial 41, Mound 1, Steuben site. UMMA Neg. 10896.

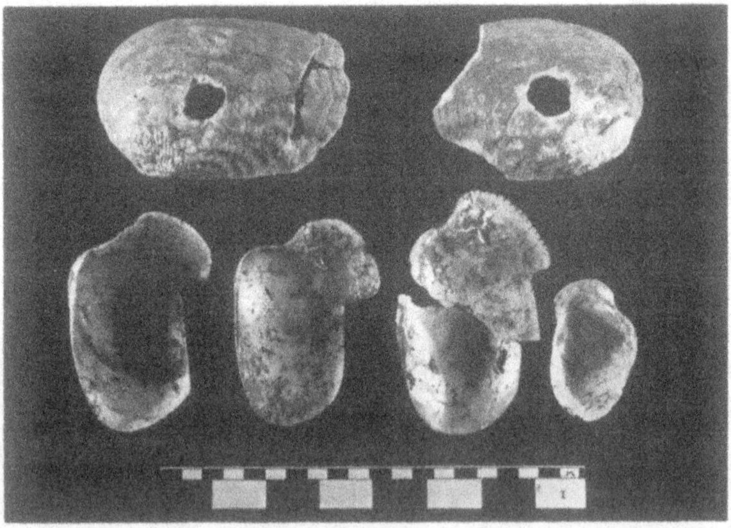

Fig. 2. Upper row: Shell hoes from Mound 1 fill. Lower row, from left to right: Shell spoons in vessel with Burial 29; in Hopewell Zoned Plain Rocked Stamped jar, Pit B; at corner of Pit B; and in vessel with Burials 39-41. UMMA Neg. 10997.

PLATE XVII

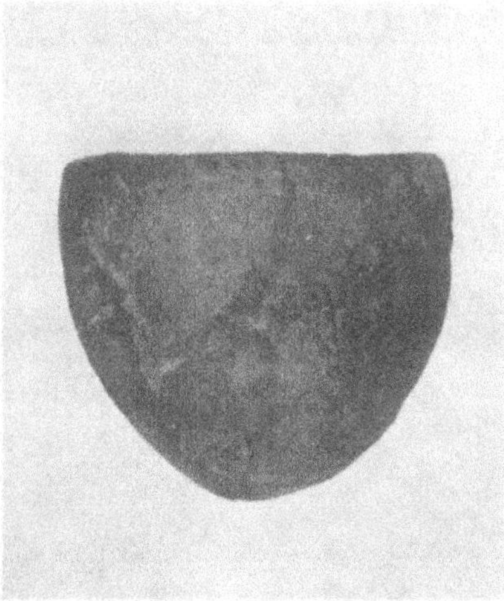

Fig. 1. Steuben Punctated vessel from Pit B, Mound 1, Steuben site. UMMA Neg. 10892.

Fig. 2. Hopewell Zoned Plain Rocked Stamped vessel from Pit B, Mound 1, Steuben site. UMMA Neg. 10890.

Fig. 3. Hopewell Zoned Plain Rocked Stamped vessel from Pit B, Mound 1, Steuben site. UMMA Neg. 11002.

PLATE XVIII

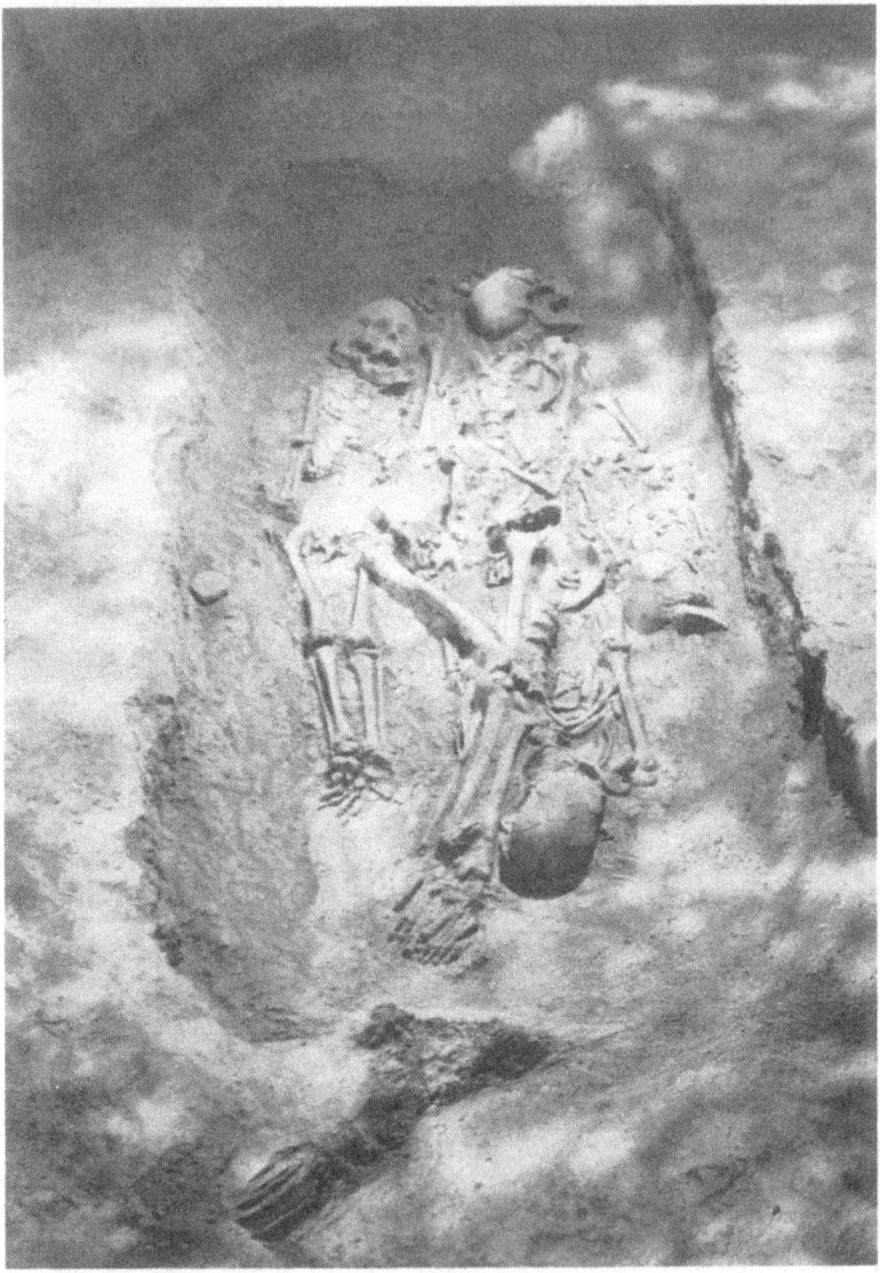

Burial Pit C, Mound 1, Steuben site. View toward northwest. Burials 31-34.

PLATE XIX

Fig. 1. Pit C, Mound 1, Steuben site. View toward southeast.

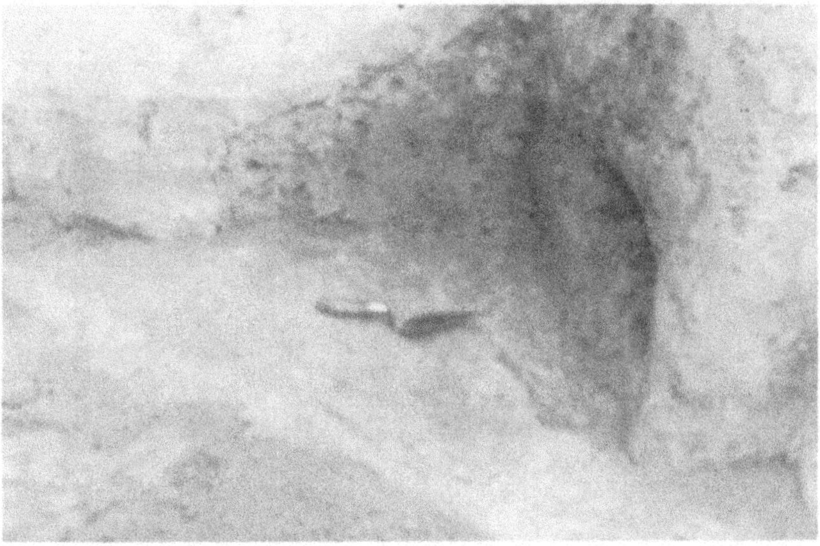

Fig. 2. Dome over Pit C, Mound 1, Steuben site. View toward southeast.

PLATE XX

Fig. 1. Baehr Zoned Brushed vessel. Associated with Burial 29, near Pit C, Mound 1, Steuben site. UMMA Neg. 10893.

Fig. 2. Burials 29-30. At edge of Pit C, Mound 1, Steuben site, toward Illinois River. View toward northeast.

PLATE XXI

Fig. 1. Pit D, Mound 1, Steuben site. View toward south.

Fig. 2. Burials 46 and 47, Pit D, Mound 1, Steuben site.

PLATE XXII

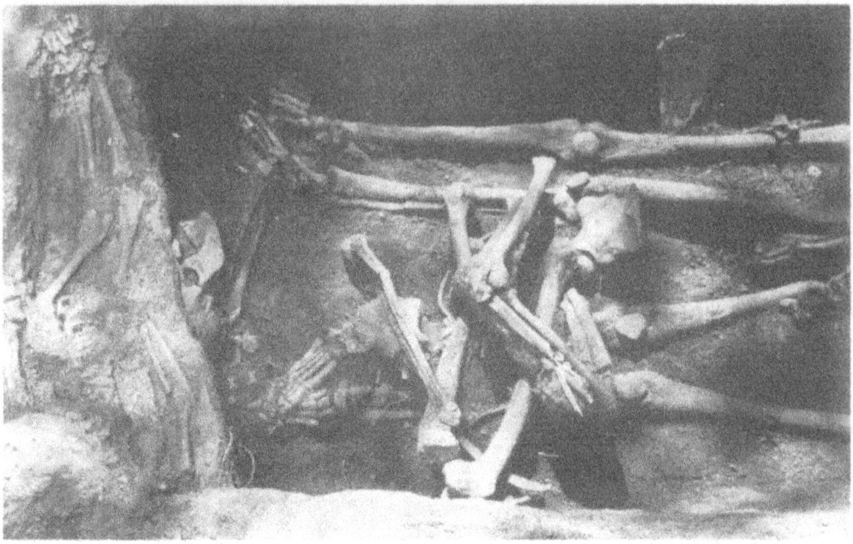

Fig. 1. Burial 45 (disarticulated), Pit D, Mound 1, Steuben site.

Fig. 2. Burials 43 and 44, Mound 1, Steuben site. Partly excavated Pit D in foreground. Log near skull (Fig. 1) is Michigan sample M-378; skull is M-380. View toward east.

PLATE XXIII

Fig. 1. Burials 39-41, Mound 1, Steuben site. View toward west.

Fig. 2. Hopewell Plain Rocked Stamped vessel. Associated with Burials 39, 40, and 41, Mound 1, Steuben site. UMMA Neg. 10895.

Fig. 3. *Busycon perversum* vessel with Burial 41, Mound 1, Steuben site. UMMA Negs. 10898 and 10899.

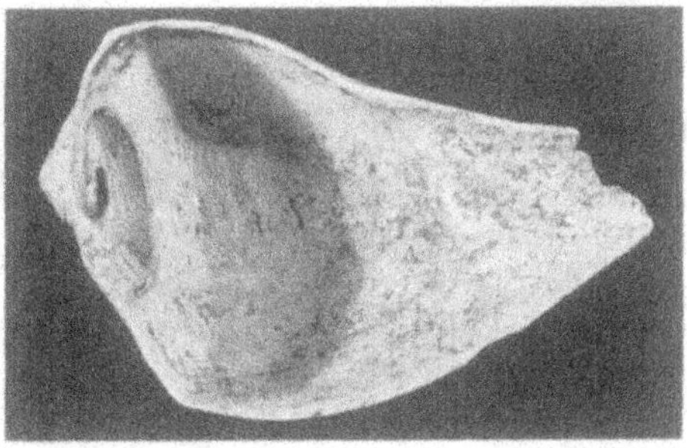

PLATE XXIV

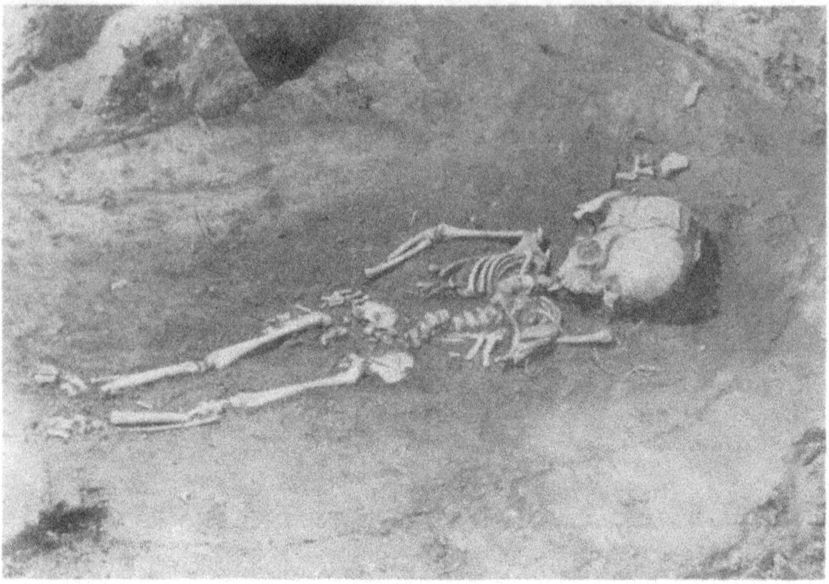

Fig. 1. Burial 42, Mound 1, Steuben site. View toward northwest.

Fig. 2. South end of Mound 1, Steuben site. Burial 37 in foreground and empty pit just north of the bundle burial group. View toward north.

PLATE XXV

Fig. 1. Burials 49-58, Mound 1, Steuben site. View toward north.

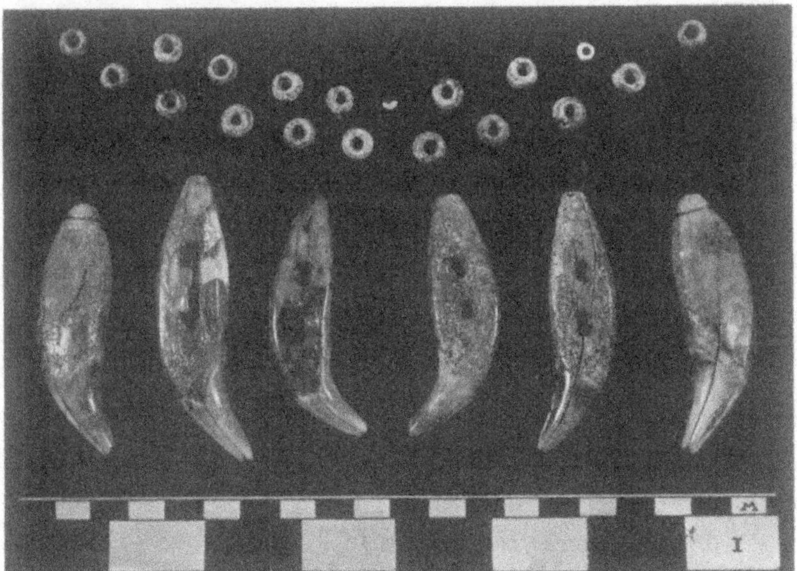

Fig. 2. Shell beads from Mound 1 fill over primary mound over Pits A and B. Grooved black bear canines associated with Burial 10. Perforated canines associated with Burial 30 near Pit C. UMMA Neg. 10900.

PLATE XXVI

Fig. 1. Shell hoe *in situ*, near Pit C, Mound 1, Steuben site.

Fig. 2. Weaver Cordmarked with notched rim. Associated with Burial 23, Mound 1, Steuben site. UMMA Neg. 11001.

PLATE XXVII

Fig. 1. Burial 24, Mound 1, Steuben site. View toward northeast.

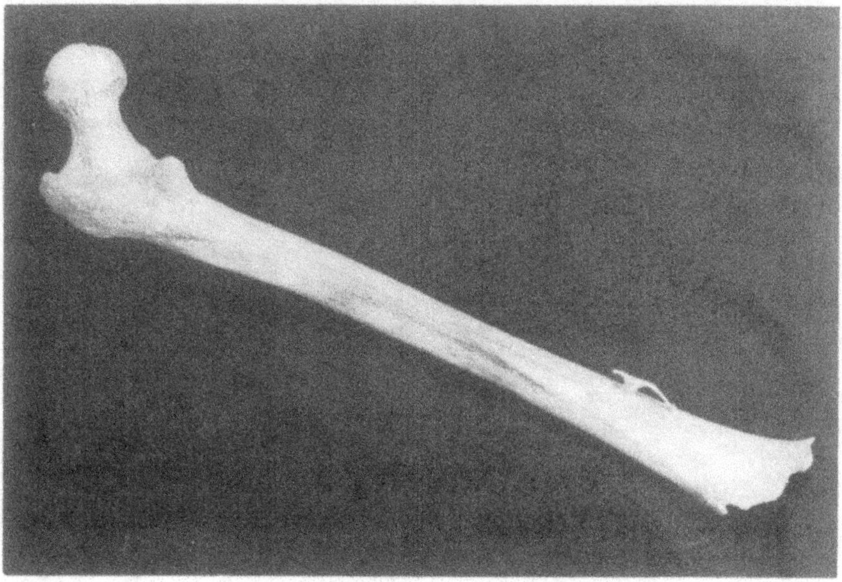

Fig. 2. The left femur of Burial 13, Mound 1, Steuben site, showing a bony spur on the posterior-medial surface of the distal end.

PLATE XXVIII

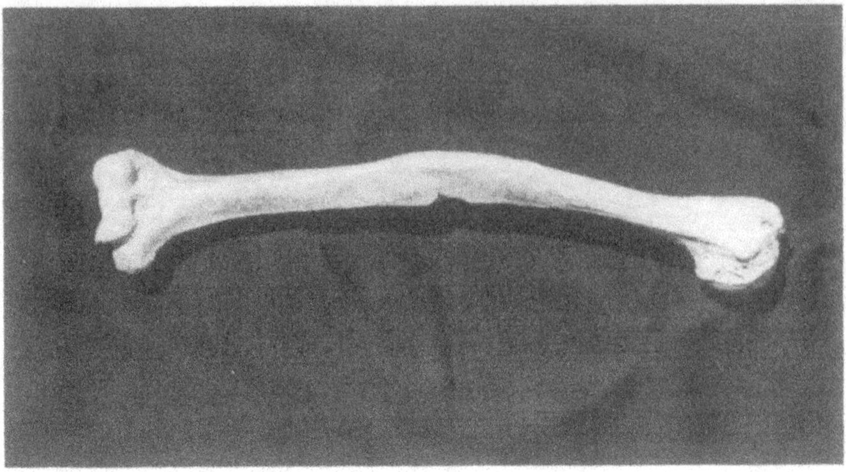

Fig. 1. The right humerus of Burial 16, Mound 1, Steuben site, showing a deformity due to a greenstick fracture.

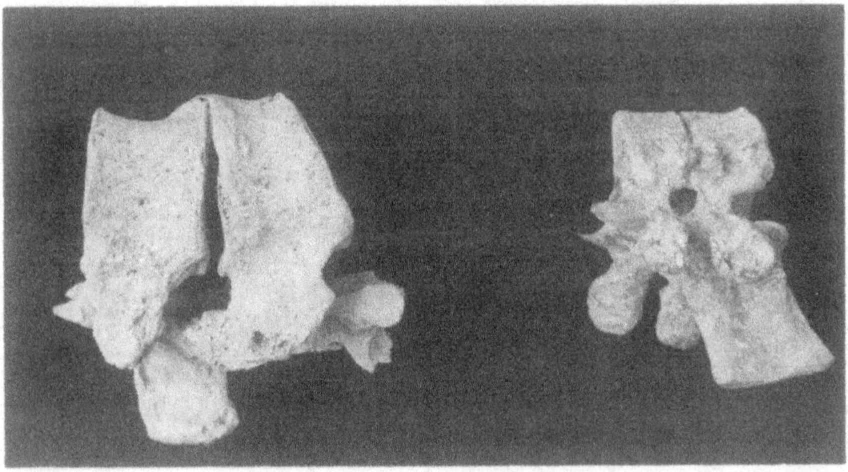

Fig. 2. Left: Twelfth thoracic and first lumbar vertebrae of Burial 37 in an ankylosed condition. Right: Fused second and third thoracic vertebrae of Burial 24. Mound 1, Steuben site.

PLATE XXIX

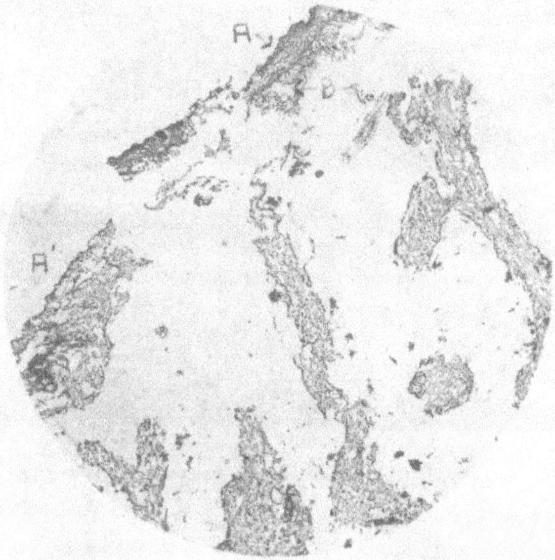

Fig. 1. Microscopic section taken through a bony growth on the distal end of first metatarsal of Burial 35, Mound 1, Steuben site.

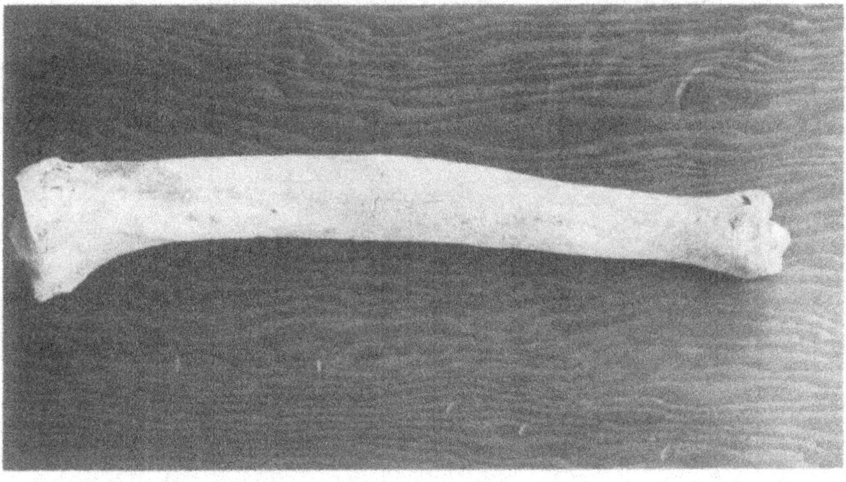

Fig. 2. Right tibia of Burial 56, Mound 1, Steuben site.

PLATE XXX

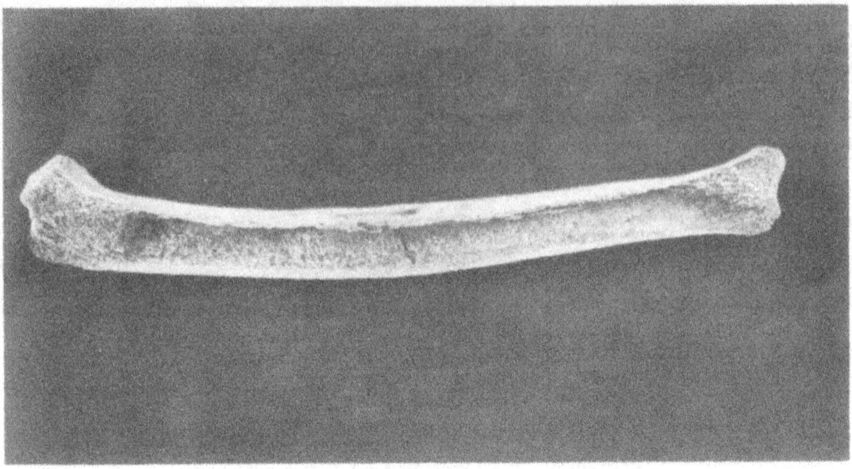

Fig. 1. Right tibia of Burial 56 sawed longitudinally.

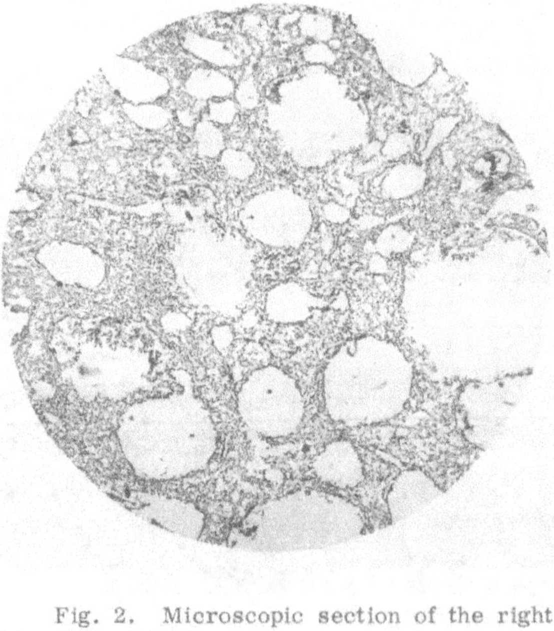

Fig. 2. Microscopic section of the right tibia of Burial 56.

PLATE XXXI

Fig. 1. Northern end of Mound 1, Steuben site. View toward south.

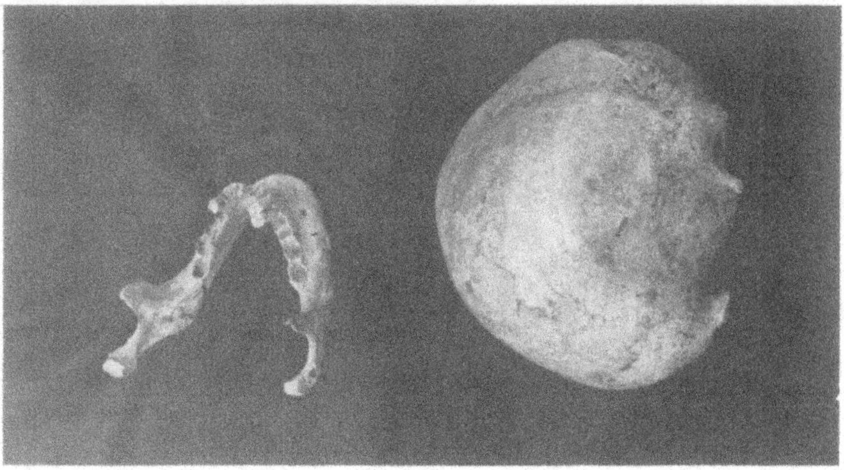

Fig. 2. Skull of Burial 49, Mound 1, Steuben site.

www.ingramcontent.com/pod-product-compliance
Lightning Source LLC
LaVergne TN
LVHW050021250826
846302LV00008B/52